TREASURY OF LIGHT COOKING

PUBLICATIONS INTERNATIONAL, LTD.

Light Cooking is a trademark of Publications International, Ltd.

Recipe Development: Sue Spitler, Incredible Edibles, Ltd., Kathleen German and Jeanne Jones

Nutritional Analysis: Linda R. Yoakam, M.S., R.D.

Photography by Sacco Productions Limited, Chicago, IL; Photo/Kevin Smith Studios, Chicago, IL and Burke/Triolo Productions/Culver City, CA.

Pictured on the front cover: Chicken and Veggie Lasagna (*page 61*).

Pictured on the back cover: Sweet and Sour Broccoli Pasta Salad (*page 94*).

ISBN: 0-7853-0899-7

Manufactured in U.S.A.

8 7 6 5 4 3 2 1

CONTENTS

Pita Pizzas (page 20)

Gazpacho Macaroni Salad (page 90)

Tempting Apple Trifles (page 228)

LESSONS IN SMART EATING

Today, people everywhere are more aware than ever before about the importance of maintaining a healthful lifestyle. In addition to proper exercise, this includes eating foods that are lower in fat, sodium and cholesterol. The goal of *Treasury of Light Cooking* is to provide today's cook with easy-to-prepare recipes that taste great, yet easily fit into your dietary goals. Eating well is a matter of making smarter choices about the foods you eat. Preparing the recipes in *Treasury of Light Cooking* is your first step toward making smart choices a delicious reality.

A Balanced Diet

The U.S. Department of Agriculture and the Department of Health and Human Services have developed a Food Guide Pyramid to illustrate how easy it is to eat a healthier diet. It is not a rigid prescription, but rather a general guide that lets you choose a healthful diet that's right for you. It calls for eating a wide variety of foods to get the nutrients you need and, at the same time, the right amount of calories to maintain a healthy weight.

Food Guide Pyramid
A Guide to Daily Food Choices

Fats, Oils, & Sweets
Use Sparingly
(Also found in other groups; see text.)

KEY
•Fat (naturally occurring and added)   ▼Sugar (added)
These symbols show fats, oils, and added sugars in foods.

Milk, Yogurt, & Cheese Group
2–3 Servings

Meat, Poultry, Fish, Dry Beans, Eggs, & Nuts Group
2–3 Servings

Vegetable Group
3–5 Servings

Fruit Group
2–4 Servings

Bread, Cereal, Rice, & Pasta Group
6–11 Servings

The number of servings, and consequently, the number of calories a person can eat each day, is determined by a number of factors, including age, weight, height, activity level and gender. Sedentary women and some older adults need about 1,600 calories each day. For most children, teenage girls, active women and many sedentary men 2,000 calories is about right. Teenage boys, active men and some very active women use about 2,800 calories each day. Use the chart below to determine how many servings you need for your calorie level.

Personalized Food Group Servings for Different Calorie Levels*			
	1,600	2,000	2,800
Bread Group Servings	6	8	11
Vegetable Group Servings	3	4	5
Fruit Group Servings	2	3	4
Milk Group Servings	2–3**	2–3**	2–3**
Meat Group Servings (ounces)	5	6	7

  * Numbers may be rounded.
  ** Women who are pregnant or breast-feeding, teenagers and young adults to age 24
     need 3 or more servings.

Lower Fat for Healthier Living

It is widely known that most Americans' diets are too high in fat. A low fat diet reduces your risk of getting certain diseases and helps you maintain a healthy weight. Studies have shown that eating more than the recommended amount of fat (especially saturated fat) is associated with increased blood cholesterol levels in some adults. A high blood cholesterol level is associated with increased risk for heart disease. A high fat diet may also increase your chances for obesity and some types of cancer.

Nutrition experts recommend diets that contain 30% or less of total daily calories from fat. The "30% calories from fat" goal applies to a total diet over time, not to a single food, serving of a recipe or meal. To find the approximate percentage of calories from fat use this easy 3-step process:

1 Multiply the grams of fat per serving by 9 (there are 9 calories in each gram of fat), to give you the number of calories from fat per serving.

2 Divide by the total number of calories per serving.

3 Multiply by 100%.

For example, imagine a 200 calorie sandwich that has 10 grams of fat.
To find the percentage of calories from fat, first multiply the grams of fat by 9: $10 \times 9 = 90$

Then, divide by the total number of calories in a serving: $90 \div 200 = .45$

Multiply by 100% to get the percentage of calories from fat: $45 \times 100\% = 45\%$

You may find doing all this math tiresome, so an easier way to keep track of the fat in your diet is to calculate the total *grams* of fat appropriate to your caloric intake, then keep a running count of fat grams over the course of a day. The Nutrition Reference Chart on page 239 lists recommended daily fat intakes based on calorie level.

Defining "Fat Free"

It is important to take the time to read food labels carefully. For example, you'll find many food products on the grocery store shelves making claims such as "97% fat free." This does not necessarily mean that 97% of the *calories* are free from fat (or that only 3 percent of calories come from fat). Often these numbers are calculated by weight. This means that out of 100 grams of this food, 3 grams are fat. Depending on what else is in the food, the percentage of calories from fat can be quite high. You may find that the percent of calories *from fat* can be as high as 50%.

Daily Values

Fat has become the focus of many diets and eating plans. This is because most Americans' diets are too high in fat. However, there are other important nutrients to be aware of, including saturated fat, sodium, cholesterol, protein, carbohydrates and several vitamins and minerals. Daily values for these nutrients have been established by the government and reflect current nutritional recommendations for a 2,000 calorie reference diet. They are appropriate for most adults and children (age 4 or older) and provide excellent guidelines for an overall healthy diet. The chart on page 239 gives the daily values for 11 different items.

Nutritional Analysis

Every recipe in *Treasury of Light Cooking* is followed by a nutritional analysis block that lists certain nutrient values for a single serving.

■   The analysis of each recipe includes all the ingredients that are listed in that recipe, *except* ingredients labeled as "optional" or "for garnish."

■   If a range is given in the yield of a recipe ("Makes 6 to 8 servings" for example), the *lower* yield was used to calculate the per serving information.

■ If a range is offered for an ingredient ("¼ to ⅛ teaspoon" for example), the *first* amount given was used to calculate the nutrition information.

■ If an ingredient is presented with an option ("2 cups hot cooked rice or noodles" for example), the *first* item listed was used to calculate the nutritional information.

■ Foods shown in photographs on the same serving plate and offered as "serve with" suggestions at the end of a recipe are *not* included in the recipe analysis unless they are listed in the ingredient list.

■ Meat should be trimmed of all visible fat since this is reflected in the nutritional analysis.

■ In recipes calling for cooked rice or noodles, the analysis was based on rice or noodles that were prepared without added salt or fat unless otherwise mentioned in the recipe.

The nutrition information that appears with each recipe was calculated by an independent nutrition consulting firm. Every effort has been made to check the accuracy of these numbers. However, because numerous variables account for a wide range of values in certain foods, all analyses that appear in this book should be considered approximate.

The recipes in this publication are *not* intended as a medically therapeutic program, nor as a substitute for medically approved diet plans for people on fat, cholesterol or sodium restricted diets. You should consult your physician before beginning any diet plan. The recipes offered here can be a part of a healthy lifestyle that meets recognized dietary guidelines. A healthy lifestyle includes not only eating a balanced diet, but engaging in proper exercise as well.

All the ingredients called for in these recipes are generally available in large supermarkets, so there is no need to go to specialty or health food stores. You'll also see an ever-increasing amount of reduced fat and nonfat products available in local markets. Take advantage of these items to reduce your daily fat intake even more.

Cooking Healthier

When cooking great-tasting low fat meals, you will find some techniques or ingredients are different from traditional cooking. Fat serves as a flavor enhancer and gives foods a distinctive and desirable texture. In order to compensate for the lack of fat and still give great-tasting results, many of the *Treasury of Light Cooking* recipes call for a selection of herbs or a combination of fresh vegetables. A wide variety of grains and pastas are also used. Many of the recipes call for alternative protein sources, such as dried beans or tofu. Often meat is included in a recipe as an accent flavor rather than the star attraction. Vegetables are often "sautéed" in a small amount of broth rather than oil. Applesauce may be added to baked goods to give a texture similar to full fat foods. These are all simple changes that you can easily make when you start cooking healthy!

Chicken Baked in Parchment (page 84)

SANDWICHES & SNACKS

THE CALIFORNIAN

❖

Alfalfa sprouts add a delicate nutty flavor plus crunchy goodness to these open-faced sandwiches. Sprouts are low in calories and fat free. Purchase sprouts that are moist and crisp; refrigerate and use within a few days of purchase.

❖

3 tablespoons reduced fat cream cheese, softened
1 tablespoon chutney
4 slices pumpernickel bread
4 lettuce leaves
¾ pound thinly sliced chicken breast (from deli)
1⅓ cups alfalfa sprouts
1 medium mango, peeled and sliced
1 pear, cored and sliced
4 strawberries

1 Combine cream cheese and chutney in small bowl; spread about 1 tablespoon on each bread slice. Place 1 lettuce leaf over cream cheese mixture. Divide chicken evenly; place over lettuce.

2 Arrange alfalfa sprouts over chicken; arrange mango and pear slices over sprouts. Garnish each open-faced sandwich with a strawberry.   *Makes 4 servings*

Nutrients per Serving:

Calories	318
(17% of calories from fat)	
Total Fat	6 g
Saturated Fat	2 g
Cholesterol	72 mg
Sodium	304 mg
Carbohydrate	36 g
Dietary Fiber	6 g
Protein	30 g
Calcium	69 mg
Iron	2 mg
Vitamin A	239 RE
Vitamin C	45 mg

DIETARY EXCHANGES:
1 Starch/Bread, 3 Lean Meat, 1½ Fruit

❖

Cook's Tip

To easily peel and slice a mango, simply place the fruit on a cutting board with one of the ends pointing toward you. Slice vertically down either side of the pit. Use a paring knife to remove the peel from the fruit. Cut the fruit away from the pit; then, cut the fruit into slices.

❖

GRILLED CHICKEN BREAST AND PEPERONATA SANDWICHES

❖

Peperonata is an Italian mixture of sweet peppers, onions and garlic cooked in olive oil. Look for peppers that are firm, thick-fleshed and bright in color. Peppers contain twice as much vitamin C as oranges and are high in vitamin A and fiber. One-half cup of raw pieces contains only 14 calories.

❖

1 tablespoon olive oil or vegetable oil
1 medium red bell pepper, sliced into strips
1 medium green bell pepper, sliced into strips
¾ cup onion slices (about 1 medium)
2 cloves garlic, minced
¼ teaspoon salt
¼ teaspoon black pepper
4 boneless skinless chicken breast halves (about 1 pound)
4 small French rolls, split and toasted

1 Heat oil in large nonstick skillet over medium heat until hot. Add bell peppers, onion and garlic; cook and stir 5 minutes. Reduce heat to low; cook and stir about 20 minutes or until vegetables are very soft. Sprinkle with salt and black pepper.

2 Grill chicken, on covered grill over medium-hot coals, 10 minutes on each side or until chicken is no longer pink in center. Or, broil chicken, 6 inches from heat source, 7 to 8 minutes on each side or until chicken is no longer pink in center.

3 Place chicken in rolls. Divide pepper mixture evenly; spoon over chicken.

Makes 4 servings

Nutrients per Serving:

Calories	321
(22% of calories from fat)	
Total Fat	8 g
Saturated Fat	2 g
Cholesterol	58 mg
Sodium	497 mg
Carbohydrate	36 g
Dietary Fiber	3 g
Protein	27 g
Calcium	48 mg
Iron	2 mg
Vitamin A	28 RE
Vitamin C	36 mg

DIETARY EXCHANGES:
2 Starch/Bread, 2½ Lean
Meat, 1½ Vegetable

❖

Cook's Tip
Using a skillet with a nonstick finish lets you cook food without sticking while using much less oil or margarine. Most nonstick finishes are dishwasher safe, but remember to use nonmetal utensils while cooking to prevent scratching the surface.

❖

BUFFALO CHICKEN TENDERS

❖

With just a few easy changes, this favorite appetizer is updated to fit into today's healthy eating plan. Chicken tenders are marinated in hot sauce and then baked, rather than fried, in this low fat version. Cool off these spicy chicken chunks by dunking them in a low fat blue cheese dressing.

❖

3 tablespoons Louisiana-style hot sauce
½ teaspoon paprika
¼ teaspoon ground red pepper
1 pound chicken tenders
½ cup fat free blue cheese dressing
¼ cup reduced fat sour cream
2 tablespoons crumbled blue cheese
1 medium red bell pepper, cut into ½-inch slices

1 Preheat oven to 375°F. Combine hot sauce, paprika and ground red pepper in small bowl; brush on all surfaces of chicken. Place chicken in greased 11 × 7-inch baking pan. Cover; marinate in refrigerator 30 minutes.

2 Bake, uncovered, about 15 minutes or until chicken is no longer pink in center.

3 Combine blue cheese dressing, sour cream and blue cheese in small serving bowl. Garnish as desired. Serve with chicken and bell pepper for dipping.

Makes 10 servings

Nutrients per Serving:	
Calories	83
(27% of calories from fat)	
Total Fat	2 g
Saturated Fat	1 g
Cholesterol	27 mg
Sodium	180 mg
Carbohydrate	5 g
Dietary Fiber	0 g
Protein	9 g
Calcium	14 mg
Iron	<1 mg
Vitamin A	19 RE
Vitamin C	7 mg

DIETARY EXCHANGES:
½ Starch/Bread, 1 Lean Meat

❖

Health Note

Eating hot and spicy foods may actually be beneficial! Capsaicinoids, which are what actually produce the burning sensation in the mouth, work as anticoagulants, possibly helping to prevent heart attacks or strokes caused by blood clots.

❖

MEDITERRANEAN SANDWICHES

❖

*Oregano grows in
abundance on the
Mediterranean hillsides and
fills the air with fragrance.
Literally translated, oregano
means "joy of the
mountain." It is related
to two other herbs,
marjoram and thyme.
These and other dried herbs
should be stored in a cool,
dark place for no more than
six months.*

❖

Nonstick cooking spray
1¼ pounds chicken tenders, cut crosswise in half
1 large tomato, cut into bite-size pieces
½ small cucumber, seeded and sliced
½ cup sweet onion slices (about 1 small)
2 tablespoons cider vinegar
1 tablespoon olive oil or vegetable oil
3 teaspoons minced fresh oregano *or* ½ teaspoon dried oregano leaves
2 teaspoons minced fresh mint *or* ⅛ teaspoon dried mint leaves
¼ teaspoon salt
12 lettuce leaves (optional)
6 whole wheat pita breads, cut crosswise in half

1 Spray large nonstick skillet with cooking spray; heat over medium heat until hot. Add chicken; cook and stir 7 to 10 minutes or until browned and no longer pink in center. Cool slightly.

2 Combine chicken, tomato, cucumber and onion in medium bowl. Drizzle with vinegar and oil; toss to coat. Sprinkle with oregano, mint and salt; toss to combine.

3 Place 1 lettuce leaf in each pita bread half, if desired. Divide chicken mixture evenly; spoon into pita bread halves.

Makes 6 servings

Nutrients per Serving:

Calories	242
(21% of calories from fat)	
Total Fat	6 g
Saturated Fat	1 g
Cholesterol	50 mg
Sodium	353 mg
Carbohydrate	24 g
Dietary Fiber	2 g
Protein	23 g
Calcium	57 mg
Iron	2 mg
Vitamin A	30 RE
Vitamin C	7 mg

DIETARY EXCHANGES:
1½ Starch/Bread, 2½ Lean
Meat

TARRAGON CHICKEN SALAD SANDWICHES

Fresh grapes are added to this chicken salad for a burst of flavor and nutritional value. Besides supplying fiber and vitamin A, grapes are low in calories, which makes them a great snack food. Green grapes that have a tinge of yellow and red grapes that are predominantly crimson will be the sweetest.

1¼ pounds boneless skinless chicken breasts, cooked
1 cup thinly sliced celery
1 cup seedless red or green grapes, cut into halves
½ cup raisins
½ cup plain nonfat yogurt
¼ cup reduced fat mayonnaise or salad dressing
2 tablespoons finely chopped shallots or onion
2 tablespoons minced fresh tarragon *or* 1 teaspoon dried tarragon leaves
½ teaspoon salt
⅛ teaspoon white pepper
6 lettuce leaves
6 whole wheat buns, split

1 Cut chicken into scant ½-inch pieces. Combine chicken, celery, grapes and raisins in large bowl. Combine yogurt, mayonnaise, shallots, tarragon, salt and pepper in small bowl. Spoon over chicken mixture; mix lightly.

2 Place 1 lettuce leaf in each bun. Divide chicken mixture evenly; spoon into buns.

Makes 6 servings

Nutrients per Serving:

Calories	353
(18% of calories from fat)	
Total Fat	7 g
Saturated Fat	1 g
Cholesterol	76 mg
Sodium	509 mg
Carbohydrate	41 g
Dietary Fiber	4 g
Protein	34 g
Calcium	120 mg
Iron	2 mg
Vitamin A	62 RE
Vitamin C	6 mg

DIETARY EXCHANGES:
1½ Starch/Bread, 4 Lean Meat, ½ Fruit

Health Tip
Be sure to read the ingredient list first before purchasing whole wheat bread products. The first ingredient listed should be *whole* wheat flour, not wheat flour. Whole wheat flour contains the wheat germ, which increases the fiber and overall nutritional content of the final product.

PITA PIZZAS

Pita, or pocket bread, is a flat bread served throughout the Middle East, either as an accompaniment to meals, stuffed to form sandwiches, or cut into wedges to serve as dippers. Using whole wheat pita breads as the chewy crust for these mini-pizzas provides an extra boost of vitamins, minerals and fiber.

Nonstick cooking spray
½ pound boneless skinless chicken breasts, cut into ½-inch cubes
½ cup thinly sliced red bell pepper
½ cup thinly sliced mushrooms
½ cup thinly sliced red onion (about 1 small)
2 cloves garlic, minced
1 teaspoon dried basil leaves
½ teaspoon dried oregano leaves
1 cup torn fresh spinach leaves
6 mini whole wheat pita breads
½ cup (2 ounces) shredded part-skim mozzarella cheese
1 tablespoon grated Parmesan cheese

1 Preheat oven to 375°F. Spray medium nonstick skillet with cooking spray; heat over medium heat until hot. Add chicken; cook and stir 6 minutes or until browned and no longer pink in center. Remove chicken from skillet.

2 Spray same nonstick skillet again with cooking spray; add bell pepper, mushrooms, onion, garlic, basil and oregano. Cook and stir over medium heat 5 to 7 minutes or until vegetables are crisp-tender. Return chicken to skillet; stir well.

3 Place spinach on top of pita breads. Divide chicken and vegetable mixture evenly; spoon over spinach. Sprinkle evenly with mozzarella and Parmesan cheese. Bake, uncovered, 7 to 10 minutes or until cheese is melted.   *Makes 6 servings*

3 points

Nutrients per Serving:

Calories	158
(17% of calories from fat)	
Total Fat	3 g
Saturated Fat	2 g
Cholesterol	125 mg
Sodium	198 mg
Carbohydrate	19 g
Dietary Fiber	4 g
Protein	14 g
Calcium	119 mg
Iron	2 mg
Vitamin A	99 RE
Vitamin C	21 mg

DIETARY EXCHANGES:
1 Starch/Bread, 1½ Lean Meat, ½ Vegetable

MEATBALL GRINDERS

❖

When purchasing ground chicken, be sure to check the label. Some brands are primarily ground from white meat. Others add dark meat and skin, which increases the fat and cholesterol content dramatically. You can also ask your butcher to grind breast meat for you.

❖

Nutrients per Serving:

Calories	340
(17% of calories from fat)	
Total Fat	7 g
Saturated Fat	2 g
Cholesterol	63 mg
Sodium	702 mg
Carbohydrate	40 g
Dietary Fiber	3 g
Protein	31 g
Calcium	121 mg
Iron	3 mg
Vitamin A	94 RE
Vitamin C	16 mg

DIETARY EXCHANGES:
2 Starch/Bread, 3 Lean
Meat, 1½ Vegetable

1 pound ground chicken
½ cup fresh whole wheat or white bread crumbs (1 slice bread)
1 egg white
3 tablespoons finely chopped fresh parsley
2 cloves garlic, minced
¼ teaspoon salt
⅛ teaspoon pepper
  Nonstick cooking spray
¼ cup chopped onion
1 can (8 ounces) whole tomatoes, drained and coarsely chopped
1 can (4 ounces) reduced sodium tomato sauce
1 teaspoon dried Italian seasoning
4 small hard rolls, split
2 tablespoons grated Parmesan cheese

1 Combine chicken, bread crumbs, egg white, parsley, garlic, salt and pepper in medium bowl. Form mixture into 12 to 16 meatballs. Spray medium nonstick skillet with cooking spray; heat over medium heat until hot. Add meatballs; cook and stir about 5 minutes or until browned on all sides. Remove meatballs from skillet.

2 Add onion to skillet; cook and stir 2 to 3 minutes. Stir in tomatoes, tomato sauce and Italian seasoning; heat to a boil. Reduce heat to low and simmer, covered, 15 minutes. Return meatballs to skillet; simmer, covered, 15 minutes.

3 Place 3 to 4 meatballs in each roll. Divide sauce evenly; spoon over meatballs. Sprinkle with cheese.
Makes 4 servings

7 points

CHICKEN AND MOZZARELLA MELTS

❖

Mozzarella is a soft white cheese that melts easily. In southern Italy, where it originated, it is made from the milk of buffaloes. In other parts of Italy and North America, it is made from cow's milk.

❖

Nutrients per Serving:

Calories	299
(16% of calories from fat)	
Total Fat	5 g
Saturated Fat	3 g
Cholesterol	47 mg
Sodium	498 mg
Carbohydrate	37 g
Dietary Fiber	3 g
Protein	27 g
Calcium	188 mg
Iron	3 mg
Vitamin A	198 RE
Vitamin C	24 mg

DIETARY EXCHANGES:
2 Starch/Bread, 2½ Lean
Meat, 1 Vegetable

 2 cloves garlic, crushed
 4 boneless skinless chicken breast halves (¾ pound)
    Nonstick cooking spray
 ⅛ teaspoon salt
 ⅛ teaspoon pepper
 1 tablespoon prepared pesto sauce
 4 small hard rolls, split
12 fresh spinach leaves
 8 fresh basil leaves* (optional)
 3 plum tomatoes, sliced
 ½ cup (2 ounces) shredded part-skim mozzarella cheese

1 Preheat oven to 350°F. Rub garlic on all surfaces of chicken. Spray medium nonstick skillet with cooking spray; heat over medium heat until hot. Add chicken; cook 5 to 6 minutes on each side or until no longer pink in center. Sprinkle with salt and pepper.

2 Brush pesto sauce on bottom halves of rolls; layer with spinach, basil, if desired, and tomatoes. Place chicken in rolls; sprinkle cheese evenly over chicken. (If desired, sandwiches may be prepared up to this point and wrapped in aluminum foil. Refrigerate until ready to bake. Bake in preheated 350°F oven until chicken is warm, about 20 minutes.)

3 Wrap sandwiches in aluminum foil; bake about 10 minutes or until cheese is melted.   *Makes 4 servings*

*Omit basil leaves if fresh are unavailable. Do not substitute dried basil leaves.

SALADS

CHICKEN AND COUSCOUS SALAD

❖

A staple of North African cuisine, couscous is a quick-cooking grain with many uses. It can be served with milk as a cereal, in casseroles or stuffings, or tossed with dressing for a salad, as it is here.

❖

1 can (14½ ounces) low sodium chicken broth, defatted
½ teaspoon ground cinnamon
¼ teaspoon ground nutmeg
¼ teaspoon curry powder
1 cup uncooked couscous
1½ pounds boneless skinless chicken breasts, cooked
2 cups fresh pineapple chunks
2 cups cubed seeded cucumber chunks
2 cups cubed red bell pepper
2 cups cubed yellow bell pepper
1 cup sliced celery
½ cup sliced green onions with tops
3 tablespoons apple cider vinegar
3 tablespoons water
2 tablespoons vegetable oil
1 tablespoon fresh mint *or* 1 teaspoon dried mint leaves
  Lettuce leaves

1 In nonstick Dutch oven or large nonstick saucepan, heat chicken broth, cinnamon, nutmeg and curry powder to a boil. Stir in couscous; remove pan from heat and let stand, covered, 5 minutes. Fluff couscous with fork; cool to room temperature.

2 Cut chicken into ½-inch pieces. Add chicken, pineapple, cucumber, bell peppers, celery and green onions to couscous; toss to combine.

3 In small jar with tight-fitting lid, combine vinegar, water, oil and mint; shake well. Pour over couscous mixture; toss to coat. Serve immediately in lettuce-lined bowl. Garnish as desired.

Makes 6 servings

Nutrients per Serving:

Calories	348
(20% of calories from fat)	
Total Fat	8 g
Saturated Fat	1 g
Cholesterol	58 mg
Sodium	85 mg
Carbohydrate	43 g
Dietary Fiber	9 g
Protein	27 g
Calcium	59 mg
Iron	2 mg
Vitamin A	143 RE
Vitamin C	150 mg

DIETARY EXCHANGES:
1½ Starch/Bread, 2½ Lean Meat, ½ Fruit,
2½ Vegetable

CHICKEN SALAD NIÇOISE

"Niçoise" refers to the cooking style of Nice, located in southern France. This main-dish salad substitutes chicken for the traditional tuna, but the integral ingredients of tomatoes, beans and potatoes remain.

Nonstick cooking spray
1 pound chicken tenders
½ cup red onion wedges (about 1 small)
Fresh spinach leaves (optional)
2 cups whole green beans, cooked and chilled
2 cups cubed red potatoes, cooked and chilled
2 cups halved cherry tomatoes
1 can (15½ ounces) Great Northern beans, drained and rinsed
Herb and Mustard Dressing (recipe follows)

1 Spray medium nonstick skillet with cooking spray; heat over medium heat until hot. Add chicken; cook and stir 7 to 10 minutes or until chicken is browned and no longer pink in center. Cool slightly; refrigerate until chilled.

2 Spray small nonstick skillet with cooking spray; heat over medium heat until hot. Add onion; cook and stir over low heat about 15 minutes or until onions are caramelized. Cool to room temperature.

3 Place spinach, if desired, on plates. Top with chicken, onions, green beans, potatoes, tomatoes and Great Northern beans. Drizzle with Herb and Mustard Dressing. Serve immediately. *Makes 6 servings*

HERB AND MUSTARD DRESSING

¼ cup water
3 tablespoons balsamic or cider vinegar
1½ tablespoons Dijon-style mustard
1 tablespoon olive oil
1 teaspoon dried basil leaves
1 teaspoon dried thyme leaves
1 teaspoon dried rosemary
1 small clove garlic, minced

1 In small jar with tight-fitting lid, combine all ingredients; shake well. Refrigerate until ready to use; shake before using. *Makes about ⅔ cup*

Nutrients per Serving:

Calories	301
(16% of calories from fat)	
Total Fat	5 g
Saturated Fat	1 g
Cholesterol	40 mg
Sodium	103 mg
Carbohydrate	42 g
Dietary Fiber	3 g
Protein	23 g
Calcium	104 mg
Iron	4 mg
Vitamin A	85 RE
Vitamin C	27 mg

DIETARY EXCHANGES:
2 Starch/Bread, 2 Lean Meat, 1½ Vegetable

BLACKENED CHICKEN SALAD

A cool and creamy yet low fat ranch salad dressing, along with chunks of crisp zucchini and cucumber, provides a refreshing contrast to spicy strips of skinless chicken.

Nutrients per Serving:

includes Ranch Salad Dressing

Calories	249
(25% of calories from fat)	
Total Fat	7 g
Saturated Fat	1 g
Cholesterol	59 mg
Sodium	369 mg
Carbohydrate	21 g
Dietary Fiber	5 g
Protein	27 g
Calcium	137 mg
Iron	5 mg
Vitamin A	664 RE
Vitamin C	45 mg

DIETARY EXCHANGES:
1 Starch/Bread, 2½ Lean
Meat, 1½ Vegetable

2 cups cubed sourdough or French bread
   Nonstick cooking spray
1 tablespoon paprika
1 teaspoon onion powder
1 teaspoon garlic powder
½ teaspoon dried oregano leaves
½ teaspoon dried thyme leaves
½ teaspoon white pepper
½ teaspoon ground red pepper
½ teaspoon black pepper
1 pound boneless skinless chicken breasts
4 cups bite-size pieces fresh spinach leaves
2 cups bite-size pieces romaine lettuce
2 cups cubed zucchini
2 cups cubed seeded cucumber
½ cup sliced green onion with tops
1 medium tomato, cut into 8 wedges
   Ranch Salad Dressing (recipe page 32)

1 Preheat oven to 375°F. To make croutons, spray bread cubes lightly with cooking spray; place in 15 × 10-inch jelly-roll pan. Bake 10 to 15 minutes or until browned, stirring occasionally.

2 Combine paprika, onion powder, garlic powder, oregano, thyme, white pepper, red pepper and black pepper in small bowl; rub on all surfaces of chicken. Broil chicken, 6 inches from heat source, 7 to 8 minutes on each side or until chicken is no longer pink in center. Or, grill chicken, on covered grill over medium-hot coals, 10 minutes on each side or until chicken is no longer pink in center. Cool slightly. Cut chicken into thin strips.

3 Combine warm chicken, greens, zucchini, cucumber, green onions, tomato and croutons in large bowl. Drizzle with Ranch Salad Dressing; toss to coat. Serve immediately.
Makes 4 servings

(continued on page 32)

Blackened Chicken Salad, continued

RANCH SALAD DRESSING

¼ cup water

3 tablespoons reduced calorie cucumber-ranch salad dressing

1 tablespoon reduced fat mayonnaise or salad dressing

1 tablespoon lemon juice

2 teaspoons minced fresh parsley

⅛ teaspoon salt

⅛ teaspoon pepper

1 In small jar with tight-fitting lid, combine all ingredients; shake well. Refrigerate until ready to use; shake before using.   *Makes about ½ cup*

❖

Cook's Tip

Cooking methods often turn low fat food into a high fat dish simply
by using oil for cooking or to prevent sticking to the pan. Naturally low
in fat, skinless chicken breasts remain that way by broiling
or grilling.

❖

CHICKEN, TORTELLINI AND ROASTED VEGETABLE SALAD

❖

Roasting vegetables at high heat gives them a wonderful new flavor complexity without adding any fat. Combine them with low fat tortellini and tender chicken to make this a vitamin-rich salad.

❖

Nutrients per Serving:

includes Sun-Dried Tomato and Basil Vinaigrette

Calories	210
(27% of calories from fat)	
Total Fat	7 g
Saturated Fat	1 g
Cholesterol	31 mg
Sodium	219 mg
Carbohydrate	24 g
Dietary Fiber	3 g
Protein	16 g
Calcium	137 mg
Iron	4 mg
Vitamin A	851 RE
Vitamin C	53 mg

DIETARY EXCHANGES:
1 Starch/Bread, 1½ Lean Meat, 1½ Vegetable, ½ Fat

3 cups whole medium mushrooms
2 cups cubed zucchini
2 cups cubed eggplant
¾ cup red onion wedges (about 1 medium)
  Nonstick olive oil cooking spray
1½ packages (9-ounce size) reduced fat cheese tortellini
6 cups bite-size pieces leaf lettuce and arugula
1 pound boneless skinless chicken breasts, cooked and cut into 1½-inch pieces
  Sun-Dried Tomato and Basil Vinaigrette (recipe page 34)

1 Heat oven to 425°F. Place mushrooms, zucchini, eggplant and onion in 15 × 10-inch jelly-roll pan. Spray generously with cooking spray; toss to coat. Bake 20 to 25 minutes or until vegetables are browned. Cool to room temperature.

2 Cook tortellini according to package directions; drain. Cool to room temperature.

3 Combine roasted vegetables, tortellini, lettuce and chicken in large bowl. Drizzle with Sun-Dried Tomato and Basil Vinaigrette; toss to coat. Serve immediately.

Makes 8 servings

(continued on page 34)

Chicken, Tortellini and Roasted Vegetable Salad, continued

SUN–DRIED TOMATO AND BASIL VINAIGRETTE

4 sun-dried tomato halves, *not* packed in oil
   Hot water
½ cup defatted low sodium chicken broth
2 tablespoons finely chopped fresh basil *or* 2 teaspoons dried basil leaves
2 tablespoons olive oil
2 tablespoons lemon juice
2 tablespoons water
1 clove garlic, minced
¼ teaspoon salt
¼ teaspoon pepper

1 Place sun-dried tomatoes in small bowl. Pour hot water over tomatoes to cover. Let stand 10 to 15 minutes or until tomatoes are soft. Drain well; chop tomatoes.

2 In small jar with tight-fitting lid, combine tomatoes and remaining ingredients; shake well. Refrigerate until ready to use; shake before using.　*Makes about 1 cup*

❖

Cook's Tip

Look for firm eggplant with smooth skin and uniform color. Usually the smaller the eggplant, the sweeter and more tender it is. Store at room temperature for two days or refrigerate in a plastic bag up to four days.

❖

TAOS CHICKEN SALAD

❖

*Jícama, a large root
vegetable, is also referred to
as the Mexico potato. It has a
sweet, nutty flavor and a
crisp texture similar to that
of water chestnuts. Jícama is
a good source of vitamin C
and potassium.*

❖

Nutrients per Serving:

Calories	258
(19% of calories from fat)	
Total Fat	6 g
Saturated Fat	1 g
Cholesterol	37 mg
Sodium	437 mg
Carbohydrate	36 g
Dietary Fiber	6 g
Protein	18 g
Calcium	143 mg
Iron	4 mg
Vitamin A	281 RE
Vitamin C	100 mg

DIETARY EXCHANGES:
1½ Starch/Bread, 1½ Lean
Meat, ½ Fruit,
1 Vegetable

3 flour or corn tortillas, cut into ¼-inch strips
  Nonstick cooking spray
1 pound boneless skinless chicken thighs, cut into strips
6 cups bite-size pieces assorted salad greens
2 oranges, peeled and cut into segments
2 cups peeled jícama strips
1 can (15½ ounces) pinto beans, drained and rinsed
1 cup cubed red bell pepper
½ cup sliced celery
½ cup sliced green onions with tops
  Lime Vinaigrette (recipe follows)

1 Preheat oven to 350°F. Spray tortilla strips lightly with cooking spray; place in 15 × 10-inch jelly-roll pan. Bake about 10 minutes or until browned, stirring occasionally. Cool to room temperature.

2 Spray medium nonstick skillet with cooking spray; heat over medium heat until hot. Add chicken; cook and stir about 15 minutes or until no longer pink in center. Refrigerate until chilled.

3 Combine greens, oranges, jícama, beans, bell pepper, celery and green onions in large bowl; add chicken. Drizzle with Lime Vinaigrette; toss to coat. Serve immediately; garnish with tortilla strips.   *Makes 6 servings*

LIME VINAIGRETTE

3 tablespoons finely chopped fresh cilantro or parsley
3 tablespoons plain low fat yogurt
3 tablespoons orange juice
2 tablespoons lime juice
2 tablespoons white wine vinegar
2 tablespoons water
1 tablespoon sugar
1 teaspoon chili powder
½ teaspoon onion powder
½ teaspoon ground cumin

1 In small jar with tight-fitting lid, combine all ingredients; shake well. Refrigerate until ready to use; shake before using.   *Makes about ¾ cup*

Soups & Stews

WHITE BEAN CHILI

❖

In addition to being an excellent source of fiber, legumes (beans, lentils and peas) are also beneficial in lowering blood cholesterol and protecting against colon cancer. Rinse and drain canned beans before using to eliminate excess sodium.

❖

Nonstick cooking spray
1 pound ground chicken
3 cups coarsely chopped celery
1½ cups coarsely chopped onions (about 2 medium)
3 cloves garlic, minced
4 teaspoons chili powder
1½ teaspoons ground cumin
¾ teaspoon ground allspice
¾ teaspoon ground cinnamon
½ teaspoon pepper
1 can (16 ounces) whole tomatoes, undrained and coarsely chopped
1 can (15½ ounces) Great Northern beans, drained and rinsed
2 cups defatted low sodium chicken broth

1 Spray large nonstick skillet with cooking spray; heat over medium heat until hot. Add chicken; cook and stir until browned, breaking into pieces with fork. Remove chicken; drain fat from skillet.

2 Add celery, onions and garlic to skillet; cook and stir over medium heat 5 to 7 minutes or until tender. Sprinkle with chili powder, cumin, allspice, cinnamon and pepper; cook and stir 1 minute.

3 Return chicken to skillet. Stir in tomatoes with juice, beans and chicken broth; heat to a boil. Reduce heat to low and simmer, uncovered, 15 minutes. Garnish as desired.

Makes 6 entree servings

Nutrients per Serving:	
Calories	232
(22% of calories from fat)	
Total Fat	6 g
Saturated Fat	1 g
Cholesterol	36 mg
Sodium	241 mg
Carbohydrate	26 g
Dietary Fiber	3 g
Protein	20 g
Calcium	117 mg
Iron	3 mg
Vitamin A	128 RE
Vitamin C	21 mg

DIETARY EXCHANGES:
1 Starch/Bread, 2 Lean Meat, 2 Vegetable

CHICKEN CACCIATORE

❖

Cacciatore is an Italian word that refers to foods prepared "hunter-style" — a naturally healthy way of cooking with mushrooms, onions, tomatoes and various herbs. This classic chicken dish is served over spaghetti, a good source of complex carbohydrates.

❖

Nutrients per Serving:

Calories	472
(30% of calories from fat)	
Total Fat	16 g
Saturated Fat	4 g
Cholesterol	107 mg
Sodium	470 mg
Carbohydrate	42 g
Dietary Fiber	4 g
Protein	40 g
Calcium	68 mg
Iron	4 mg
Vitamin A	153 RE
Vitamin C	69 mg

DIETARY EXCHANGES:
2½ Starch/Bread, 4½ Lean Meat, 1½ Vegetable, ½ Fat

Nonstick cooking spray
4 pounds chicken pieces (breasts, legs, thighs)
2 cups sliced mushrooms
2 cups chopped green bell peppers
¾ cup coarsely chopped onion (about 1 medium)
3 cloves garlic, minced
1 can (16 ounces) whole tomatoes, undrained and coarsely chopped
¾ cup tomato juice
½ cup water
¼ cup tomato paste
1 tablespoon sugar
2 teaspoons dried rosemary
1 teaspoon dried basil leaves
1 teaspoon dried oregano leaves
½ teaspoon salt
¼ teaspoon black pepper
6 cups hot cooked spaghetti

1 Generously spray nonstick Dutch oven or large nonstick skillet with cooking spray; heat over medium heat until hot. Cook chicken 10 to 15 minutes or until browned on all sides. Drain fat from Dutch oven.

2 Add mushrooms, bell peppers, onion and garlic to Dutch oven; cook and stir 3 to 4 minutes.

3 Stir in canned tomatoes with juice, ¾ cup tomato juice, water, tomato paste, sugar, rosemary, basil, oregano, salt and black pepper; heat to a boil. Reduce heat to low and simmer, covered, 45 minutes. Uncover; simmer about 30 minutes or until chicken is no longer pink in center and juices run clear. Serve over spaghetti. Garnish as desired.

Makes 8 entree servings

CHICKEN AND CORN CHOWDER

❖

This hearty chowder is thickened in a healthful way. A portion of the ingredients are processed in a blender until finely chopped, then added to the rest of the chowder. As a result, milk can be used instead of heavy cream to finish the soup, saving over 30 grams of fat per serving.

❖

Nonstick cooking spray
1 pound boneless skinless chicken breasts, cut into ½-inch pieces
3 cups thawed frozen whole kernel corn
¾ cup coarsely chopped onion (about 1 medium)
1 to 2 tablespoons water
1 cup diced carrots
2 tablespoons finely chopped jalapeño pepper
½ teaspoon dried oregano leaves
¼ teaspoon dried thyme leaves
3 cups defatted low sodium chicken broth
1½ cups 2% milk
½ teaspoon salt

1 Spray large nonstick saucepan with cooking spray; heat over medium heat until hot. Add chicken; cook and stir about 10 minutes or until browned and no longer pink in center. Remove chicken from saucepan.

2 Add corn and onion to saucepan; cook and stir about 5 minutes or until onion is tender. Place 1 cup corn mixture in food processor or blender. Process until finely chopped, adding 1 to 2 tablespoons water to liquify mixture; reserve.

3 Add carrots, jalapeño pepper, oregano and thyme to saucepan; cook and stir about 5 minutes or until corn begins to brown. Return chicken to saucepan. Stir in chicken broth, milk, reserved corn mixture and salt; heat to a boil. Reduce heat to low and simmer, covered, 15 to 20 minutes.

Makes 4 entree servings

Nutrients per Serving:	
Calories	292
(14% of calories from fat)	
Total Fat	5 g
Saturated Fat	2 g
Cholesterol	65 mg
Sodium	465 mg
Carbohydrate	36 g
Dietary Fiber	4 g
Protein	29 g
Calcium	151 mg
Iron	2 mg
Vitamin A	874 RE
Vitamin C	9 mg

DIETARY EXCHANGES:
1½ Starch/Bread, 2½ Lean Meat, ½ Milk, ½ Vegetable

4 points

GREEK-STYLE CHICKEN STEW

❖

This stew is ideal for the health-conscious way we eat today. It boasts plenty of authentic Greek flavor with eggplant, artichokes and oregano, yet it has just over 350 calories per serving.

❖

Nutrients per Serving:

Calories	353
(14% of calories from fat)	
Total Fat	5 g
Saturated Fat	1 g
Cholesterol	117 mg
Sodium	246 mg
Carbohydrate	32 g
Dietary Fiber	7 g
Protein	41 g
Calcium	76 mg
Iron	4 mg
Vitamin A	29 RE
Vitamin C	10 mg

DIETARY EXCHANGES:
1½ Starch/Bread, 3½ Lean Meat, 2 Vegetable

3 pounds skinless chicken breasts
  Flour
  Nonstick cooking spray
2 cups cubed peeled eggplant
2 cups sliced mushrooms
¾ cup coarsely chopped onion (about 1 medium)
2 cloves garlic, minced
1 teaspoon dried oregano leaves
½ teaspoon dried basil leaves
½ teaspoon dried thyme leaves
2 cups defatted low sodium chicken broth
¼ cup dry sherry *or* defatted low sodium chicken broth
¼ teaspoon salt
¼ teaspoon pepper
1 can (14 ounces) artichoke hearts, drained
3 cups hot cooked wide egg noodles

1 Coat chicken very lightly with flour. Generously spray nonstick Dutch oven or large nonstick skillet with cooking spray; heat over medium heat until hot. Cook chicken 10 to 15 minutes or until browned on all sides. Remove chicken; drain fat from Dutch oven.

2 Add eggplant, mushrooms, onion, garlic, oregano, basil and thyme to Dutch oven; cook and stir over medium heat 5 minutes.

3 Return chicken to Dutch oven. Stir in chicken broth, sherry, salt and pepper; heat to a boil. Reduce heat to low and simmer, covered, about 1 hour or until chicken is no longer pink in center and juices run clear, adding artichoke hearts during last 20 minutes of cooking. Serve over noodles. Garnish as desired.

Makes 6 entree servings

MEXICAN TORTILLA SOUP

Fresh cilantro is used extensively in Mexican cooking. Also called fresh coriander or Chinese parsley, this pungent herb is similar in appearance to flat-leaf parsley.

Nutrients per Serving:

Calories	184
(15% of calories from fat)	
Total Fat	3 g
Saturated Fat	1 g
Cholesterol	58 mg
Sodium	132 mg
Carbohydrate	16 g
Dietary Fiber	4 g
Protein	23 g
Calcium	66 mg
Iron	2 mg
Vitamin A	1,595 RE
Vitamin C	41 mg

DIETARY EXCHANGES:
2½ Lean Meat, 2 Vegetable

Nonstick cooking spray
2 pounds boneless skinless chicken breasts, cut into ½-inch strips
4 cups diced carrots
2 cups sliced celery
1 cup chopped green bell pepper
1 cup chopped onion (about 1 large)
4 cloves garlic, minced
1 teaspoon dried oregano leaves
½ teaspoon ground cumin
1 jalapeño pepper, sliced and seeded
8 cups defatted low sodium chicken broth
1 large tomato, seeded and chopped
4 to 5 tablespoons lime juice
2 (6-inch) corn tortillas, cut into ¼-inch strips
Salt (optional)
3 tablespoons finely chopped cilantro

1 Preheat oven to 350°F. Spray large nonstick saucepan with cooking spray; heat over medium heat until hot. Add chicken; cook and stir about 10 minutes or until browned and no longer pink in center. Add carrots, celery, bell pepper, onion, garlic, oregano, cumin and jalapeño pepper; cook and stir over medium heat 5 minutes.

2 Stir in chicken broth, tomato and lime juice; heat to a boil. Reduce heat to low and simmer, covered, 15 to 20 minutes.

3 Meanwhile, spray tortilla strips lightly with cooking spray; sprinkle very lightly with salt, if desired. Place on baking sheet. Bake about 10 minutes or until browned and crisp, stirring occasionally.

4 Stir cilantro into soup. Ladle soup into bowls; top with tortilla strips.

Makes 8 entree servings

3 points

CHICKEN FRICASSEE

❖

This main-dish stew combines three favorites— hearty chicken, crunchy carrots and tender pasta. A low fat white sauce made with chicken broth, milk and flour gets a delicious flavor boost from dill.

❖

Nutrients per Serving:

Calories	565
(30% of calories from fat)	
Total Fat	19 g
Saturated Fat	5 g
Cholesterol	158 mg
Sodium	357 mg
Carbohydrate	52 g
Dietary Fiber	6 g
Protein	43 g
Calcium	110 mg
Iron	4 mg
Vitamin A	2,226 RE
Vitamin C	10 mg

DIETARY EXCHANGES:
3 Starch/Bread, 4½ Lean
Meat, 2 Vegetable, 1 Fat

3 pounds chicken pieces (breasts, legs, thighs)
Flour
Nonstick cooking spray
3 cups defatted low sodium chicken broth
1 bay leaf
1 pound whole baby carrots
¾ cup onion wedges (about 1 medium)
1 tablespoon margarine
3 tablespoons flour
¾ cup skim milk
1 tablespoon lemon juice
3 tablespoons minced fresh dill *or* 2 teaspoons dried dill weed
1 teaspoon sugar
½ teaspoon salt
6 cups hot cooked noodles

1 Coat chicken pieces very lightly with flour. Spray large nonstick skillet with cooking spray; heat over medium heat until hot. Cook chicken 10 to 15 minutes or until browned on all sides. Drain fat from skillet.

2 Add chicken broth and bay leaf to skillet; heat to a boil. Reduce heat to low and simmer, covered, about 1 hour or until chicken is no longer pink in center and juices run clear, adding carrots and onion during last 20 minutes of cooking.

3 Transfer chicken and vegetables with slotted spoon to platter; keep warm. Heat broth to a boil; boil until broth is reduced to 1 cup. Discard bay leaf.

4 Melt margarine in small saucepan over low heat; stir in 3 tablespoons flour. Cook and stir 1 to 2 minutes. Stir in broth, milk and lemon juice; heat to a boil. Boil until thickened, stirring constantly. Stir in dill, sugar and salt. Arrange chicken over noodles on serving plates; top with sauce. Garnish as desired.

Makes 6 entree servings

10 points

CHICKEN BOURGUIGNONNE

❖

Wild rice is actually the seed of a marsh grass rather than a type of rice. Its nutty flavor and chewy texture make it a perfect accompaniment to all kinds of poultry. A half cup of cooked wild rice has about ten times the amount of folic acid as white rice.

Folic acid is a nutrient important for the formation and growth of red blood cells.

❖

Nutrients per Serving:	
Calories	396
(18% of calories from fat)	
Total Fat	8 g
Saturated Fat	2 g
Cholesterol	92 mg
Sodium	251 mg
Carbohydrate	36 g
Dietary Fiber	4 g
Protein	35 g
Calcium	62 mg
Iron	4 mg
Vitamin A	1,639 RE
Vitamin C	14 mg

DIETARY EXCHANGES:
2 Starch/Bread, 3½ Lean Meat, 2½ Vegetable

4 pounds skinless chicken thighs and breasts
Flour
Nonstick cooking spray
2 cups defatted low sodium chicken broth
2 cups dry white wine or defatted low sodium chicken broth
1 pound whole baby carrots
¼ cup tomato paste
4 cloves garlic, minced
½ teaspoon dried thyme leaves
2 bay leaves
¼ teaspoon salt
¼ teaspoon pepper
8 ounces fresh or thawed frozen pearl onions
8 ounces whole medium mushrooms
2 cups hot cooked white rice
2 cups hot cooked wild rice
¼ cup minced fresh parsley

1 Preheat oven to 325°F. Coat chicken very lightly with flour. Generously spray nonstick ovenproof Dutch oven or large nonstick ovenproof skillet with cooking spray; heat over medium heat until hot. Cook chicken 10 to 15 minutes or until browned on all sides. Drain fat from Dutch oven.

2 Add chicken broth, wine, carrots, tomato paste, garlic, thyme, bay leaves, salt and pepper to Dutch oven; heat to a boil. Cover; transfer to oven. Bake 1 hour. Add onions and mushrooms. Uncover; bake about 35 minutes or until vegetables are tender and chicken is no longer pink in center and juices run clear. Remove bay leaves. Combine white and wild rice; serve with chicken. Sprinkle rice with parsley.

Makes 8 servings

8 points

ENTREES

CHICKEN CORDON BLEU

6 boneless skinless chicken breast halves (1¼ pounds)
1 tablespoon Dijon-style mustard
3 slices (1 ounce each) lean ham, cut into halves
3 slices (1 ounce each) reduced fat Swiss cheese, cut into halves
   Nonstick cooking spray
¼ cup unseasoned dry bread crumbs
2 tablespoons minced fresh parsley
3 cups hot cooked rice

1 Preheat oven to 350°F. Pound chicken breasts between 2 pieces of plastic wrap to ¼-inch thickness using flat side of meat mallet or rolling pin. Brush mustard on 1 side of each chicken breast; layer 1 slice each of ham and cheese over mustard. Roll up each chicken breast from short end; secure with wooden picks. Spray tops of chicken rolls with cooking spray; sprinkle with bread crumbs.

2 Arrange chicken rolls in 11 × 7-inch baking pan. Cover; bake 10 minutes. Uncover; bake about 20 minutes or until chicken is no longer pink in center.

3 Stir parsley into rice; serve with chicken. Serve with vegetables if desired.

Makes 6 servings

Pounding boneless chicken breasts to a uniform thickness flattens them so that a savory ham and cheese filling can be easily rolled up inside.

Nutrients per Serving:

Calories	297
(18% of calories from fat)	
Total Fat	6 g
Saturated Fat	2 g
Cholesterol	55 mg
Sodium	294 mg
Carbohydrate	32 g
Dietary Fiber	1 g
Protein	27 g
Calcium	166 mg
Iron	2 mg
Vitamin A	46 RE
Vitamin C	5 mg

DIETARY EXCHANGES:
2 Starch/Bread, 2 Lean Meat

Health Note

Boneless skinless chicken breasts are a favorite choice for today's cook because of their quick-cooking appeal and low fat, high protein content.

6 points

CHICKEN AND VEGETABLE RISOTTO

❖

Arborio rice, used in this recipe, is a type of short-grain rice grown in Italy; it can be purchased in large supermarkets and Italian groceries. If you prepare the risotto with regular converted rice, you may not need to use all of the broth.

❖

Nonstick olive oil cooking spray
2 cups sliced mushrooms
½ cup chopped onion (about 1 small)
4 cloves garlic, minced
¼ cup finely chopped fresh parsley *or* 1 tablespoon dried parsley leaves
3 to 4 tablespoons finely chopped fresh basil *or* 1 tablespoon dried basil leaves
6 cups defatted low sodium chicken broth
1½ cups uncooked arborio rice *or* converted rice
2 cups broccoli flowerettes, cooked crisp-tender
1 pound chicken tenders, cut into ½-inch pieces and cooked
4 plum tomatoes, seeded and chopped
½ teaspoon salt
½ teaspoon pepper
2 tablespoons grated Parmesan or Romano cheese

1 Spray large nonstick saucepan with cooking spray; heat over medium heat until hot. Add mushrooms, onion and garlic; cook and stir about 5 minutes or until tender. Add parsley and basil; cook and stir 1 minute.

2 Heat chicken broth to a boil in medium saucepan. Reduce heat to low; simmer.

3 Add rice to mushroom mixture; cook and stir over medium heat 1 to 2 minutes. Add chicken broth to mushroom mixture, ½ cup at a time, stirring constantly until broth is absorbed before adding next ½ cup. Continue adding broth and stirring until rice is tender and mixture is creamy, 20 to 25 minutes.

4 Add broccoli, chicken, tomatoes, salt and pepper. Cook and stir 2 to 3 minutes or until heated through. Sprinkle with cheese.   *Makes 4 servings*

8 points

Nutrients per Serving:

Calories	457
(9% of calories from fat)	
Total Fat	5 g
Saturated Fat	1 g
Cholesterol	48 mg
Sodium	449 mg
Carbohydrate	74 g
Dietary Fiber	5 g
Protein	29 g
Calcium	153 mg
Iron	7 mg
Vitamin A	225 RE
Vitamin C	90 mg

DIETARY EXCHANGES:
4 Starch/Bread, 2 Lean Meat, 2½ Vegetable

GRILLED CHICKEN WITH SOUTHERN BARBECUE SAUCE

Grilling—and its indoor counterpart, broiling—is a very healthy cooking method since it allows fat to drip away from food during cooking. In any recipe calling for chicken pieces, always use tongs to turn chicken pieces while cooking. This prevents the meat from being pierced, keeping the natural juices sealed inside.

Nonstick cooking spray
½ cup chopped onion (about 1 small)
4 cloves garlic, minced
1 can (16 ounces) no-salt-added tomato sauce
¾ cup water
3 tablespoons firmly packed light brown sugar
3 tablespoons chili sauce
2 teaspoons chili powder
2 teaspoons dried thyme leaves
2 teaspoons white Worcestershire sauce
¾ teaspoon ground red pepper
½ teaspoon ground cinnamon
½ teaspoon black pepper
6 skinless chicken breast halves (2¼ pounds)
6 medium Idaho potatoes, baked, hot

1 Spray medium nonstick skillet with cooking spray; heat over medium heat until hot. Add onion and garlic; cook and stir about 5 minutes or until tender. Stir in tomato sauce, water, sugar, chili sauce, chili powder, thyme, Worcestershire sauce, red pepper, cinnamon and black pepper; heat to a boil. Reduce heat to low and simmer, uncovered, 30 minutes or until mixture is reduced to 1½ cups. Pour ¾ cup sauce into small bowl for basting; reserve.

2 Grill chicken, on covered grill over medium-hot coals, 40 to 45 minutes or until chicken is no longer pink in center and juices run clear, turning chicken several times and basting occasionally with reserved sauce.

3 Heat remaining sauce in skillet over medium heat until hot; spoon over chicken. Serve with potatoes. Serve with additional vegetables, if desired.

Makes 6 servings

Nutrients per Serving:

Calories	357
(8% of calories from fat)	
Total Fat	3 g
Saturated Fat	1 g
Cholesterol	69 mg
Sodium	218 mg
Carbohydrate	51 g
Dietary Fiber	5 g
Protein	30 g
Calcium	61 mg
Iron	3 mg
Vitamin A	132 RE
Vitamin C	11 mg

DIETARY EXCHANGES:
2 Starch/Bread, 3 Lean Meat, 2 Vegetable

RICOTTA STUFFED CHICKEN WITH SUN-DRIED TOMATO LINGUINE

❖

Sun-dried tomatoes are a new addition to many supermarket produce departments. These chewy tomatoes have a sweet taste and add a rich tomato flavor to soups, stews and sauces.

❖

Nutrients per Serving:

includes Sun-Dried Tomato Linguine

Calories	529
(26% of calories from fat)	
Total Fat	15 g
Saturated Fat	4 g
Cholesterol	135 mg
Sodium	232 mg
Carbohydrate	54 g
Dietary Fiber	4 g
Protein	45 g
Calcium	150 mg
Iron	5 mg
Vitamin A	1,590 RE
Vitamin C	35 mg

DIETARY EXCHANGES:
3 Starch/Bread, 4½ Lean
Meat, 2 Vegetable,
½ Fat

1 broiler-fryer chicken (3 pounds)
1 cup reduced fat ricotta cheese
1 cup chopped fresh spinach leaves
4 cloves garlic, minced
2 teaspoons dried basil leaves
2 teaspoons minced fresh parsley
1 teaspoon dried oregano leaves
¼ teaspoon salt
  Nonstick olive oil cooking spray
  Paprika
  Sun-Dried Tomato Linguine (recipe page 60)

1 Preheat oven to 375°F. Split chicken in half with sharp knife or poultry shears, cutting through breastbone. Place chicken, skin side up, on counter and press with palm of hand to crack bone so that chicken will lie flat.

2 Loosen skin over top of chicken using fingers and sharp paring knife; do not loosen skin over wings and drumsticks.

3 Combine ricotta cheese, spinach, garlic, basil, parsley, oregano and salt in small bowl. Stuff mixture under skin of chicken, using small rubber spatula or spoon.

4 Place chicken in roasting pan. Spray top of chicken lightly with cooking spray; sprinkle with paprika. Bake about 1 hour 15 minutes or until chicken is no longer pink in center and juices run clear. Serve with Sun-Dried Tomato Linguine. Garnish as desired.

Makes 6 servings

(continued on page 60)

Ricotta Stuffed Chicken With Sun-Dried Tomato Linguine, continued

SUN–DRIED TOMATO LINGUINE

6 sun-dried tomato halves, *not* packed in oil
  Hot water
  Nonstick olive oil cooking spray
1 cup sliced mushrooms
3 cloves garlic, minced
1 tablespoon minced fresh parsley
¾ teaspoon dried rosemary
1 can (15 ounces) low sodium chicken broth, defatted
2 tablespoons cornstarch
¼ cup cold water
1 package (9 ounces) linguine, cooked in salted water, drained, hot

1 Place sun-dried tomatoes in small bowl; pour hot water over to cover. Let stand 10 to 15 minutes or until tomatoes are soft. Drain well; cut tomatoes into quarters.

2 Spray medium nonstick skillet with cooking spray; heat over medium heat until hot. Add mushrooms and garlic; cook and stir about 5 minutes or until tender. Add sun-dried tomatoes, parsley and rosemary; cook and stir 1 minute.

3 Stir chicken broth into vegetable mixture; heat to a boil. Combine cornstarch and cold water in small bowl; stir into chicken broth mixture. Boil 1 to 2 minutes, stirring constantly. Pour mixture over linguine; toss to coat.   *Makes 6 servings*

CHICKEN AND VEGGIE LASAGNA

Pasta is a great source of complex carbohydrates. It also contains six essential amino acids, three B-complex vitamins and iron. When cooking pasta, make sure the water is at a rolling boil. This circulates the pasta so that it cooks evenly.

Tomato-Herb Sauce (recipe page 62)
Nonstick olive oil cooking spray
1½ cups thinly sliced zucchini
1 cup thinly sliced carrots
3 cups torn fresh spinach leaves
½ teaspoon salt
1 package (15 ounces) fat free ricotta cheese
½ cup grated Parmesan cheese
9 lasagna noodles, cooked and drained
2 cups (8 ounces) reduced fat shredded mozzarella cheese

1 Prepare Tomato-Herb Sauce.

2 Preheat oven to 350°F. Spray large nonstick skillet with cooking spray; heat over medium heat until hot. Add zucchini and carrots; cook and stir about 5 minutes or until almost tender. Remove from heat; stir in spinach and salt.

3 Combine ricotta and Parmesan cheese in small bowl. Spread 1¾ cups Tomato-Herb Sauce on bottom of 13 × 9-inch baking pan. Top with 3 noodles. Spoon half the ricotta cheese mixture over noodles; spread lightly with spatula. Spoon half the zucchini mixture over ricotta cheese mixture; sprinkle with 1 cup mozzarella cheese. Repeat layers; place remaining 3 noodles on top.

4 Spread remaining Tomato-Herb Sauce over noodles. Cover with aluminum foil; bake 1 hour or until sauce is bubbly. Let stand 5 to 10 minutes; cut into rectangles. Garnish as desired.

Makes 12 servings

5 points

Nutrients per Serving:

includes Tomato-Herb Sauce

Calories	254
(27% of calories from fat)	
Total Fat	8 g
Saturated Fat	2 g
Cholesterol	51 mg
Sodium	431 mg
Carbohydrate	26 g
Dietary Fiber	4 g
Protein	22 g
Calcium	154 mg
Iron	3 mg
Vitamin A	480 RE
Vitamin C	29 mg

DIETARY EXCHANGES:
1 Starch/Bread, 2 Lean Meat, 2 Vegetable, ½ Fruit

(continued on page 62)

Chicken and Veggie Lasagna, continued

TOMATO–HERB SAUCE

    Nonstick olive oil cooking spray
1½ cups chopped onions (about 2 medium)
 4 cloves garlic, minced
 1 tablespoon dried basil leaves
 1 teaspoon dried oregano leaves
 ½ teaspoon dried tarragon leaves
 ¼ teaspoon dried thyme leaves
2½ pounds ripe tomatoes, peeled and cut into wedges
 1 pound ground chicken, cooked, crumbled, drained
 ¾ cup water
 ¼ cup no-salt-added tomato paste
 ½ teaspoon salt
 ½ teaspoon pepper

1 Spray large nonstick skillet with cooking spray; heat over medium heat until hot. Add onions, garlic, basil, oregano, tarragon and thyme; cook and stir about 5 minutes or until onions are tender.

2 Add tomatoes, chicken, water and tomato paste; heat to a boil. Reduce heat to low and simmer, uncovered, about 20 minutes or until sauce is reduced to 5 cups. Stir in salt and pepper.

Makes 5 cups

❖

Health Note

Recent studies have shown that eating generous amounts of garlic may play a role in protection against heart disease. Results indicate that garlic may cause serum cholesterol levels to drop, help prevent blood clots that lead to heart attacks and strokes and aid in lowering blood pressure.

❖

TEX-MEX CHICKEN

❖

Boneless skinless chicken breasts are a favorite choice for today's cook because of their quick-cooking appeal and their low fat, high protein content. If you skin and debone your own chicken breasts, save the bones and skin in a plastic bag in your freezer to make flavorful homemade chicken stock.

❖

1 teaspoon ground red pepper
¾ teaspoon onion powder
¾ teaspoon garlic powder
½ teaspoon dried basil leaves
½ teaspoon salt, divided
⅛ teaspoon dried oregano leaves
⅛ teaspoon dried thyme leaves
⅛ teaspoon gumbo filé powder*
6 boneless skinless chicken breast halves (1½ pounds)
¾ pound potatoes, cut into 1-inch wedges
   Nonstick cooking spray
¼ teaspoon black pepper

1 Combine ground red pepper, onion powder, garlic powder, basil, ¼ teaspoon salt, oregano, thyme and gumbo filé powder in small bowl. Rub mixture on all surfaces of chicken. Place chicken in single layer in 13 × 9-inch baking pan. Refrigerate, covered, 4 to 8 hours.

2 Preheat oven to 350°F. Place potatoes in medium bowl. Spray potatoes lightly with cooking spray; toss to coat. Sprinkle with remaining ¼ teaspoon salt and black pepper; toss to combine. Add to chicken in pan.

3 Bake, uncovered, 40 to 45 minutes or until potatoes are tender and chicken is no longer pink in center. Or, grill chicken and potatoes, in aluminum foil pan, on covered grill over medium-hot coals, 20 to 30 minutes or until potatoes are tender and chicken is no longer pink in center. Serve with additional vegetables, if desired.

Makes 6 servings

*Gumbo filé powder is a seasoning widely used in Creole cooking. It is available in the spice or gourmet section of most large supermarkets.

5 points

Nutrients per Serving:

Calories	262
(9% of calories from fat)	
Total Fat	3 g
Saturated Fat	1 g
Cholesterol	55 mg
Sodium	237 mg
Carbohydrate	36 g
Dietary Fiber	0 g
Protein	24 g
Calcium	25 mg
Iron	2 mg
Vitamin A	18 RE
Vitamin C	23 mg

DIETARY EXCHANGES:
1 Starch/Bread, 2 Lean Meat

CHICKEN FAJITAS

The name of this popular Southwestern dish actually refers to the strips of marinated and grilled skirt steak that are wrapped inside the warmed tortillas. This chicken version eliminates over 80 calories and 10 grams of fat per serving. The vitamin C content soars thanks to lots of crisp-tender bell peppers.

Nutrients per Serving:

Calories	382
(17% of calories from fat)	
Total Fat	7 g
Saturated Fat	2 g
Cholesterol	60 mg
Sodium	421 mg
Carbohydrate	51 g
Dietary Fiber	5 g
Protein	29 g
Calcium	134 mg
Iron	4 mg
Vitamin A	119 RE
Vitamin C	159 mg

DIETARY EXCHANGES:
2 Starch/Bread, 3 Lean Meat, 3 Vegetable

7 points/2 fajita

1 pound chicken tenders
¼ cup lime juice
4 cloves garlic, minced, divided
  Nonstick cooking spray
1 cup sliced red bell peppers
1 cup sliced green bell peppers
1 cup sliced yellow bell peppers
¾ cup onion slices (about 1 medium)
½ teaspoon ground cumin
¼ teaspoon salt
¼ teaspoon ground red pepper
8 teaspoons low fat sour cream
8 (6-inch) flour tortillas, warm
  Green onion tops (optional)
  Salsa (optional)

Excellent! sprinkle on fajita seasoning

1 Arrange chicken in 11×7-inch glass baking dish; add lime juice and 2 cloves minced garlic. Toss to coat. Cover; marinate in refrigerator 30 minutes, stirring occasionally.

2 Spray large nonstick skillet with cooking spray; heat over medium heat until hot. Add chicken mixture; cook and stir 5 to 7 minutes or until chicken is browned and no longer pink in center. Remove from skillet. Drain excess liquid from skillet, if necessary. *(Grill for a bit.)*

3 Add bell peppers, onion and remaining 2 cloves minced garlic to skillet; cook and stir about 5 minutes or until tender. Sprinkle with cumin, salt and ground red pepper. Return chicken to skillet. Cook and stir 1 to 2 minutes.

4 Spread 1 teaspoon sour cream on 1 side of each tortilla. Spoon chicken and pepper mixture over sour cream; roll up tortillas. Tie each tortilla with green onion top, if desired. Serve with salsa, if desired.

Makes 4 servings

CHICKEN POT PIE

❖

Tissue-thin layers of flaky phyllo dough top this pot pie replacing the usual high fat pastry crust. Phyllo dough has typically been used to make classic Greek dishes such as spanakopita and baklava, but because frozen phyllo dough is readily available in supermarkets, its use is becoming more widespread.

❖

Nutrients per Serving:

Calories	266
(17% of calories from fat)	
Total Fat	5 g
Saturated Fat	2 g
Cholesterol	59 mg
Sodium	300 mg
Carbohydrate	32 g
Dietary Fiber	5 g
Protein	23 g
Calcium	50 mg
Iron	2 mg
Vitamin A	1,061 RE
Vitamin C	19 mg

DIETARY EXCHANGES:
1½ Starch/Bread, 2½ Lean Meat, 1 Vegetable

5 points

Nonstick cooking spray
¾ pound boneless skinless chicken thighs, cut into 1-inch pieces
¾ pound boneless skinless chicken breasts, cut into 1-inch pieces
2 cups sliced carrots
1½ cups cubed potatoes
1 cup cubed turnip
1 cup fresh peas or thawed frozen peas
½ cup chopped onion (about 1 small)
3 cloves garlic, sliced
1 teaspoon dried basil leaves
½ teaspoon dried marjoram leaves
½ teaspoon dried oregano leaves
½ teaspoon dried tarragon leaves
¼ teaspoon salt
¼ teaspoon pepper
1 cup defatted low sodium chicken broth
3 tablespoons all-purpose flour
⅓ cup cold water
3 sheets thawed frozen phyllo pastry

1 Preheat oven to 425°F. Spray large nonstick skillet with cooking spray; heat over medium heat until hot. Add chicken; cook and stir about 10 minutes or until no longer pink in center. Remove chicken from skillet.

2 Add carrots, potatoes, turnip, peas, onion and garlic to skillet; cook and stir 5 minutes. Sprinkle with basil, marjoram, oregano, tarragon, salt and pepper; cook and stir 1 to 2 minutes. Stir in chicken broth; heat to a boil. Reduce heat to low and simmer, covered, about 10 minutes or until vegetables are tender.

3 Return chicken to skillet; return mixture to a boil. Combine flour and water in small bowl; stir into chicken mixture. Boil 1 minute, stirring constantly. Pour mixture into 1-quart casserole or 10-inch pie plate.

4 Spray 1 sheet phyllo with cooking spray; top with remaining 2 sheets phyllo, spraying each lightly. Place stack of phyllo on top of casserole; cut edges 1 inch larger than casserole. Fold under edges of phyllo. Bake about 15 minutes or until phyllo is brown and crisp.

Makes 6 servings

5 points

CHICKEN AND CURRIED FRUIT

❖

The intense, sweet flavor and chewy texture of dried fruit is highlighted by curry and other flavorings in this simple entrée. Leftover dried fruit may be sprinkled over cereal or tossed pilafs or stuffings. Remember that a little goes a long way— although low in fat, dried fruit is higher in calories than fresh fruit.

❖

Nutrients per Serving:	
Calories	383
(7% of calories from fat)	
Total Fat	4 g
Saturated Fat	1 g
Cholesterol	69 mg
Sodium	81 mg
Carbohydrate	52 g
Dietary Fiber	3 g
Protein	29 g
Calcium	51 mg
Iron	3 mg
Vitamin A	70 RE
Vitamin C	11 mg

DIETARY EXCHANGES:
2 Starch/Bread, 3 Lean
Meat, 1½ Fruit,
½ Vegetable

6 skinless chicken breast halves (2¼ pounds)
1 cup mixed diced dried fruit
½ cup chopped onion (about 1 small)
¼ cup chopped chutney
3 cloves garlic, minced
1 to 1½ teaspoons curry powder
1 teaspoon ground cumin
¼ teaspoon ground red pepper
¼ teaspoon ground allspice
2½ cups defatted low sodium chicken broth
⅓ cup dry sherry or apple juice
3 cups hot cooked rice or couscous

1 Preheat oven to 350°F. Arrange chicken, breast side up, in single layer in 13×9-inch baking pan. Place dried fruit around chicken. Combine onion, chutney, garlic, curry powder, cumin, red pepper and allspice in medium bowl; stir in chicken broth and sherry. Pour mixture over chicken and fruit.

2 Cover; bake 30 minutes. Uncover; bake about 15 minutes or until chicken is no longer pink in center and juices run clear.

3 Remove chicken from pan; arrange over rice on serving platter. Process half the fruit and half the liquid mixture from pan in food processor or blender until smooth; spoon over chicken. Discard remaining liquid mixture. Arrange remaining fruit over chicken.

Makes 6 servings

❖

Cook's Note

Fresh chicken is highly perishable. It can be stored in the coldest part of your refrigerator for two to three days. Once cooked, it will keep for three to four days.

❖

CHEESE RAVIOLI WITH SPINACH PESTO AND CHICKEN

❖

Pesto is a wonderful, fresh-tasting sauce that originated in Italy and is traditionally made with fresh basil leaves. Spinach is substituted in this recipe, providing a powerful punch of iron and vitamins A and C. One pound of raw spinach will yield four cups of leaves.

❖

Nutrients per Serving:

includes Cheese Ravioli and Spinach Pesto

Calories	284
(26% of calories from fat)	
Total Fat	8 g
Saturated Fat	1 g
Cholesterol	74 mg
Sodium	173 mg
Carbohydrate	28 g
Dietary Fiber	3 g
Protein	23 g
Calcium	101 mg
Iron	3 mg
Vitamin A	356 RE
Vitamin C	21 mg

DIETARY EXCHANGES:
1½ Starch/Bread, 2½ Lean
Meat, 1½ Vegetable

Cheese Ravioli (recipe page 74) *or* 2 (9-ounce) packages refrigerated low fat ravioli
Spinach Pesto (recipe page 74)
Nonstick cooking spray
¾ cup matchstick size carrot strips
¾ cup thinly sliced celery
½ cup chopped onion (about 1 small)
2 cloves garlic, minced
1 can (14½ ounces) no-salt-added stewed tomatoes
1½ pounds chicken tenders, cut crosswise into halves
¼ cup dry white wine
2 teaspoons dried rosemary
¼ teaspoon salt
⅛ teaspoon pepper

1 Prepare Cheese Ravioli and Spinach Pesto.

2 Spray large nonstick skillet with cooking spray; heat over medium heat until hot. Add carrots, celery, onion and garlic; cook and stir about 5 minutes or until crisp-tender.

3 Add tomatoes, chicken, wine, rosemary, salt and pepper; heat to a boil. Reduce heat to low and simmer, uncovered, about 10 minutes or until vegetables are tender and chicken is no longer pink in center.

4 Arrange Cheese Ravioli on serving plates; spoon chicken and vegetable mixture over ravioli. Top with Spinach Pesto or serve alongside.   *Makes 8 servings*

(continued on page 74)

Cheese Ravioli with Spinach Pesto and Chicken, continued

CHEESE RAVIOLI

Nonstick cooking spray
¼ cup finely chopped onion
2 cloves garlic, minced
2 tablespoons minced fresh parsley
½ teaspoon dried basil leaves
¼ teaspoon *each* dried oregano and dried thyme leaves
⅛ teaspoon pepper
½ cup reduced fat ricotta cheese
32 won ton wrappers
1½ quarts plus 2 tablespoons water, divided
2 teaspoons cornstarch

1 Spray small nonstick skillet with cooking spray; heat over medium heat until hot. Add onion and garlic; cook and stir 2 to 3 minutes or until tender. Sprinkle with parsley, basil, oregano, thyme and pepper; cook and stir 1 minute. Remove from heat; stir in ricotta cheese.

2 Place 2 teaspoons cheese mixture in center of each of 16 won ton wrappers. Combine 2 tablespoons water and cornstarch in small bowl; brush on edges of wrappers. Top with remaining won ton wrappers; press to seal edges.

3 Place remaining 1½ quarts water in large saucepan. Bring to a boil over medium-high heat. Boil 4 to 6 ravioli at a time, uncovered, 2 to 3 minutes or until ravioli are tender and rise to surface of water. Repeat with remaining ravioli.

Makes 8 servings (2 ravioli per serving)

SPINACH PESTO

2 cups loosely packed fresh spinach leaves
2 tablespoons grated Romano cheese
2 tablespoons olive oil or vegetable oil
1 to 2 tablespoons lemon juice
1 tablespoon dried basil leaves
3 cloves garlic, minced

1 Process all ingredients in food processor or blender until smooth.

Makes about 1 cup

TUSCAN CHICKEN BREASTS WITH POLENTA

❖

Cornmeal is ground from dried white or yellow corn and is a versatile grain high in fiber and many essential nutrients. Polenta, a staple of northern Italy, is a mush made from cornmeal. Here, it is cooled until firm, then sliced, lightly browned and topped with an herbed tomato sauce.

❖

4 cups defatted low sodium chicken broth
1 cup yellow cornmeal
½ teaspoon garlic powder
½ teaspoon dried Italian seasoning
¼ teaspoon salt
¼ teaspoon pepper
8 skinless chicken breast halves (3 pounds)
  Nonstick cooking spray
  Fresh spinach leaves, steamed (optional)
  Tuscan Tomato Sauce (recipe page 76)

1 In large nonstick saucepan, heat chicken broth to a boil; slowly stir in cornmeal. Reduce heat to low; cook, stirring frequently, 15 to 20 minutes or until mixture is very thick and pulls away from side of pan. (Mixture may be lumpy.) Pour polenta into greased 9 × 5-inch loaf pan. Cool; refrigerate 2 to 3 hours or until firm.

2 Heat oven to 350°F. Combine garlic powder, Italian seasoning, salt and pepper in small bowl; rub on all surfaces of chicken. Arrange chicken, breast side up, in single layer in 13 × 9-inch baking pan. Bake, uncovered, about 45 minutes or until chicken is no longer pink in center and juices run clear.

3 Remove polenta from pan; transfer to cutting board. Cut polenta crosswise into 16 slices. Cut slices into triangles, if desired. Spray large nonstick skillet with cooking spray; heat over medium heat until hot. Cook polenta about 4 minutes per side or until lightly browned.

4 Place spinach leaves, if desired, on serving plates. Arrange polenta slices and chicken over spinach; top with Tuscan Tomato Sauce. *Makes 8 servings*

(continued on page 76)

Tuscan Chicken Breasts with Polenta, continued

Nutrients per Serving:

includes Tuscan Tomato Sauce

Calories	240
(16% of calories from fat)	
Total Fat	4 g
Saturated Fat	1 g
Cholesterol	69 mg
Sodium	345 mg
Carbohydrate	22 g
Dietary Fiber	5 g
Protein	29 g
Calcium	51 mg
Iron	3 mg
Vitamin A	126 RE
Vitamin C	27 mg

DIETARY EXCHANGES:
1 Starch/Bread, 2½ Lean
Meat, 1½ Vegetable

4 points

TUSCAN TOMATO SAUCE

Nonstick cooking spray
½ cup chopped onion
2 cloves garlic, minced
8 plum tomatoes, coarsely chopped
1 can (8 ounces) tomato sauce
2 teaspoons dried basil leaves
2 teaspoons dried oregano leaves
2 teaspoons dried rosemary
½ teaspoon pepper

1 Spray medium nonstick saucepan with cooking spray; heat over medium heat until hot. Add onion and garlic; cook and stir about 5 minutes or until tender.

2 Stir in tomatoes, tomato sauce, basil, oregano, rosemary and pepper; heat to a boil. Reduce heat to low and simmer, uncovered, about 6 minutes or until desired consistency, stirring occasionally. *Makes about 3 cups*

❖

Cook's Tip

To easily peel garlic, place a clove on a cutting board. Cover the clove with the flat side of a chef's knife blade, then firmly press down on the blade with your fist. This loosens the skin so that it comes right off.

❖

MEDITERRANEAN CHICKEN KABOBS

❖

Although eggplant is commonly thought of as a vegetable, it is actually a fruit—specifically a berry. Eggplant is a good source of folic acid and potassium. One cup of raw eggplant pieces contains only 22 calories.

❖

Nutrients per Serving:

2 kabobs per serving

Calories	293
(23% of calories from fat)	
Total Fat	8 g
Saturated Fat	1 g
Cholesterol	46 mg
Sodium	60 mg
Carbohydrate	34 g
Dietary Fiber	7 g
Protein	22 g
Calcium	56 mg
Iron	3 mg
Vitamin A	49 RE
Vitamin C	16 mg

DIETARY EXCHANGES:
1½ Starch/Bread, 2 Lean Meat, 2 Vegetable, 1½ Fat

2 pounds boneless skinless chicken breasts or chicken tenders, cut into 1-inch pieces
1 small eggplant, cut into 1-inch pieces and peeled
1 medium zucchini, cut crosswise into ½-inch slices
2 medium onions, each cut into 8 wedges
16 medium mushrooms, stems removed
16 cherry tomatoes
1 cup defatted low sodium chicken broth
⅔ cup balsamic vinegar
3 tablespoons olive oil or vegetable oil
2 tablespoons dried mint leaves
4 teaspoons dried basil leaves
1 tablespoon dried oregano leaves
2 teaspoons grated lemon peel
   Chopped fresh parsley (optional)
4 cups hot cooked couscous

1 Alternately thread chicken, eggplant, zucchini, onions, mushrooms and tomatoes onto 16 metal skewers; place in large glass baking dish.

2 Combine chicken broth, vinegar, oil, mint, basil and oregano in small bowl; pour over kabobs. Cover; marinate in refrigerator 2 hours, turning kabobs occasionally.

3 Broil kabobs, 6 inches from heat source, 10 to 15 minutes or until chicken is no longer pink in center, turning kabobs halfway through cooking time. Or, grill kabobs, on covered grill over medium-hot coals, 10 to 15 minutes or until chicken is no longer pink in center, turning kabobs halfway through cooking time. Stir lemon peel and parsley into couscous; serve with kabobs. *Makes 8 servings*

CRISPY BAKED CHICKEN

Buy the freshest broccoli by choosing bunches that range in color from dark green to purple-green. Bud clusters should be compact, showing no yellow color. Avoid bunches with yellow, wilted leaves. Fresh or frozen, broccoli is a good source of vitamins A and C.

4 skinless chicken breast halves (1½ pounds)
2½ tablespoons Dijon-style mustard, divided
1 cup fresh whole wheat bread crumbs (2 slices bread)
½ teaspoon dried marjoram leaves
½ teaspoon dried thyme leaves
¼ teaspoon salt
¼ teaspoon dried sage leaves
¼ teaspoon black pepper
   Nonstick cooking spray
1 small red bell pepper, sliced
2 cloves garlic, minced
2 cups broccoli flowerettes, cooked crisp-tender
1 to 2 tablespoons lemon juice

1 Preheat oven to 375°F. Brush tops of chicken breasts with 2 tablespoons mustard. Combine bread crumbs, remaining ½ tablespoon mustard, marjoram, thyme, salt, sage and black pepper in small bowl. Pat mixture evenly over mustard. Arrange chicken, breast side up, in single layer in 13 × 9-inch baking pan.

2 Bake, uncovered, about 40 minutes or until chicken is no longer pink in center and juices run clear.

3 Spray medium nonstick skillet with cooking spray; heat over medium heat until hot. Add bell pepper and garlic; cook and stir about 5 minutes or until tender. Add broccoli and lemon juice; cook and stir 2 to 3 minutes or until heated through.

4 Arrange chicken and broccoli mixture on serving plates.   *Makes 4 servings*

Nutrients per Serving:

Calories	196
(18% of calories from fat)	
Total Fat	4 g
Saturated Fat	1 g
Cholesterol	69 mg
Sodium	412 mg
Carbohydrate	11 g
Dietary Fiber	3 g
Protein	29 g
Calcium	66 mg
Iron	2 mg
Vitamin A	86 RE
Vitamin C	62 mg

DIETARY EXCHANGES:
½ Starch/Bread, 2½ Lean Meat, 1 Vegetable

4 points

+

p. 150

❖

Cook's Tip

Mustard is one of the most frequently eaten condiments in the world. One variety, Dijon mustard, is smooth with a slightly hot undertone and is made in Dijon, France. Dijon-style mustard is its American counterpart.

❖

SESAME CHICKEN AND VEGETABLE STIR-FRY

❖

Start on your way toward eating five servings of fruits and vegetables a day with this delicious stir-fry, flavored with traditional Chinese spices and a touch of sesame oil. The combination of broccoli and red peppers contributes over 100% of the daily requirement of vitamin C.

❖

1 tablespoon Oriental sesame oil
1 pound chicken tenders, cut into 1-inch pieces
2 cups broccoli flowerettes
1 small red bell pepper, sliced
½ cup onion slices (about 1 small)
½ cup snow peas
1 can (8 ounces) water chestnuts, sliced and drained
2 cloves garlic, minced
1 teaspoon five-spice powder
1 cup defatted low sodium chicken broth
2 teaspoons cornstarch
2 tablespoons cold water
2 cups hot cooked rice

1 Heat sesame oil in wok or large nonstick skillet over medium heat until hot. Add chicken; stir-fry about 8 minutes or until chicken is no longer pink in center. Remove chicken from wok.

2 Add broccoli, bell pepper, onion, peas, water chestnuts and garlic to wok; stir-fry 5 to 8 minutes or until vegetables are crisp-tender. Sprinkle with five-spice powder; cook and stir 1 minute.

3 Return chicken to wok. Add chicken broth; heat to a boil. Combine cornstarch and water in small bowl; stir into broth mixture. Boil 1 to 2 minutes, stirring constantly. Serve over rice.

Makes 4 servings

Nutrients per Serving:

Calories	354
(19% of calories from fat)	
Total Fat	7 g
Saturated Fat	1 g
Cholesterol	59 mg
Sodium	83 mg
Carbohydrate	44 g
Dietary Fiber	3 g
Protein	27 g
Calcium	64 mg
Iron	3 mg
Vitamin A	89 RE
Vitamin C	71 mg

DIETARY EXCHANGES:
2 Starch/Bread, 3 Lean Meat, 2 Vegetable

❖

Cook's Tip

Oriental sesame oil is an amber-colored oil pressed from toasted sesame seeds. It has a strong, nut-like flavor and is used to accent many Oriental dishes. Sesame oil is high in polyunsaturated fats, which may help to lower blood cholesterol levels.

❖

CHICKEN BAKED IN PARCHMENT

❖

Baking in parchment paper seals in natural juices and flavorings and also eliminates the need to add fat. As the food cooks and lets off steam, the parchment puffs up into a dome shape. For a dramatic presentation at the table, carefully slit the paper and peel it back to reveal the food inside.

❖

Nutrients per Serving:

Calories	321
(9% of calories from fat)	
Total Fat	3 g
Saturated Fat	1 g
Cholesterol	58 mg
Sodium	214 mg
Carbohydrate	41 g
Dietary Fiber	3 g
Protein	28 g
Calcium	45 mg
Iron	2 mg
Vitamin A	810 RE
Vitamin C	42 mg

DIETARY EXCHANGES:
2 Starch/Bread, 2½ Lean
Meat, 1½ Vegetable

Parchment paper
4 boneless skinless chicken breast halves (4 ounces each)
1 cup matchstick size carrot strips
1 cup matchstick size zucchini strips
½ cup snow peas
½ cup thinly sliced red bell pepper
2¼ cups defatted low sodium chicken broth, divided
2 tablespoons all-purpose flour
2 cloves garlic, minced
½ teaspoon dried thyme leaves
¼ teaspoon salt
¼ teaspoon ground nutmeg
¼ teaspoon black pepper
1 package (6 ounces) wheat pilaf mix

1 Preheat oven to 375°F. Cut parchment paper into four 10-inch squares. Place 1 chicken breast in center of each piece of parchment; arrange carrots, zucchini, peas and bell pepper around chicken.

2 Combine ½ cup chicken broth and flour in small saucepan; stir in garlic, thyme, salt, nutmeg and black pepper. Heat to a boil, stirring constantly, until thickened. Reduce heat to low; simmer 1 minute. Spoon broth mixture evenly over chicken and vegetables.

3 Fold each parchment square in half diagonally, enclosing chicken and vegetables to form a triangle. Fold edges over twice to seal. Place parchment packets on 15 × 10-inch jelly-roll pan. Bake 25 to 30 minutes or until parchment is browned and puffed.

4 Place remaining 1¾ cups chicken broth in medium saucepan. Heat to a boil over medium-high heat. Stir in pilaf mix (discard spice packet). Reduce heat to low and simmer, covered, 15 minutes or until broth is absorbed.

5 Arrange parchment packets on serving plates; open carefully. Serve with pilaf.

Makes 4 servings

Pasta Primavera (page 128)

Light Cooking™

PASTA

SALADS

SALMON AND GREEN BEAN SALAD WITH PASTA

❖

All salmon are high in protein, the B vitamins, vitamin A and are also a rich source of OMEGA-3 oils, which studies show protect against heart disease.

❖

1 can (6¼ ounces) salmon
8 ounces uncooked small whole wheat or regular pasta shells
¾ cup fresh green beans, cut into 2-inch pieces
⅔ cup finely chopped carrots
½ cup nonfat cottage cheese
3 tablespoons plain nonfat yogurt
1½ tablespoons lemon juice
1 tablespoon fresh dill
2 teaspoons grated onion
1 teaspoon prepared mustard

1 Drain salmon and separate into chunks; set aside.

2 Cook pasta according to package directions, including ¼ teaspoon salt; add green beans during last 3 minutes of cooking. Drain and rinse well under cold water until pasta and green beans are cool.

3 Combine pasta, green beans, carrots and salmon in medium bowl.

4 Place cottage cheese, yogurt, lemon juice, dill, onion and mustard in blender or food processor; process until smooth. Pour over pasta mixture; toss to coat evenly. Garnish as desired.

Makes 6 (1-cup) servings

Nutrients per Serving:	
Calories	210
(15% of calories from fat)	
Total Fat	3 g
Saturated Fat	1 g
Cholesterol	15 mg
Sodium	223 mg
Carbohydrate	29 g
Dietary Fiber	2 g
Protein	16 g
Calcium	118 mg
Iron	2 mg
Vitamin A	383 RE
Vitamin C	5 mg

DIETARY EXCHANGES:
1½ Starch/Bread, 1½ Lean Meat, ½ Vegetable

GAZPACHO MACARONI SALAD

❖

Gazpacho is traditionally an uncooked soup of puréed fresh vegetables. Here we have chopped the vegetables and mixed them with macaroni; the result—a healthy and colorful array for all your senses.

❖

Nutrients per Serving:	
Calories	136
(11% of calories from fat)	
Total Fat	2 g
Saturated Fat	<1 g
Cholesterol	0 mg
Sodium	114 mg
Carbohydrate	27 g
Dietary Fiber	3 g
Protein	5 g
Calcium	33 mg
Iron	2 mg
Vitamin A	91 RE
Vitamin C	56 mg

DIETARY EXCHANGES:
1 Starch/Bread, ½ Fat,
2½ Vegetable

  4 ounces uncooked macaroni
2½ cups chopped, seeded tomatoes
  1 cup finely chopped red onion
  1 cup finely chopped cucumber
  ½ cup finely chopped celery
  ½ cup finely chopped green bell pepper
  ½ cup finely chopped red bell pepper
  3 tablespoons cider vinegar
  2 tablespoons finely chopped black olives
  1 bay leaf
  2 tablespoons minced fresh parsley *or* 1 teaspoon dried parsley
  1 tablespoon fresh thyme *or* ½ teaspoon dried thyme leaves
  1 clove garlic, minced
  3 to 4 dashes hot pepper sauce
  ¼ teaspoon ground black pepper

1 Cook pasta according to package directions, omitting salt. Drain and rinse well under cold water until pasta is cool; drain well.

2 Combine pasta and remaining ingredients in medium bowl. Cover and refrigerate 4 hours for flavors to blend. Remove bay leaf before serving. Garnish with whole olives, cucumber slices and dill sprigs, if desired. Serve chilled or at room temperature.

Makes 6 (1-cup) servings

CHICKEN CAESAR SALAD

Nutrients per Serving:	
Calories	379
(19% of calories from fat)	
Total Fat	8 g
Saturated Fat	2 g
Cholesterol	56 mg
Sodium	294 mg
Carbohydrate	45 g
Dietary Fiber	7 g
Protein	32 g
Calcium	171 mg
Iron	4 mg
Vitamin A	339 RE
Vitamin C	35 mg

DIETARY EXCHANGES:
2 Starch/Bread, 3 Lean
Meat, 3 Vegetable

4 small boneless skinless chicken breast halves
6 ounces uncooked gnocchi or other dried pasta
1 package (9 ounces) frozen artichoke hearts, thawed
1½ cups cherry tomatoes, quartered
¼ cup plus 2 tablespoons plain nonfat yogurt
2 tablespoons reduced calorie mayonnaise
2 tablespoons grated Romano cheese
1 tablespoon sherry or red wine vinegar
1 clove garlic, minced
½ teaspoon anchovy paste
½ teaspoon Dijon mustard
½ teaspoon ground white pepper
1 small head romaine lettuce, torn into bite-size pieces
1 cup toasted bread cubes

1 Grill or broil chicken breasts until no longer pink in center; set aside.

2 Cook pasta according to package directions, omitting salt. Drain and rinse well under cold water until pasta is cool; drain well. Combine pasta, artichoke hearts and tomatoes in large bowl; set aside.

3 Combine yogurt, mayonnaise, Romano cheese, sherry, garlic, anchovy paste, mustard and white pepper in small bowl; whisk until smooth. Add to pasta mixture; toss to coat evenly.

4 Arrange lettuce on platter or individual plates. Spoon pasta mixture over lettuce. Thinly slice chicken breasts and place on top of pasta. Sprinkle with bread cubes.

Makes 4 main-dish servings

SWEET AND SOUR BROCCOLI PASTA SALAD

❖

If you have shied away from sweet and sour dishes because of the high fat content, then this dish is for you! Apple juice, cider vinegar, mustard, honey and nonfat yogurt provide the taste sensations in this nutritious salad.

❖

Nutrients per Serving:	
Calories	198
(15% of calories from fat)	
Total Fat	3 g
Saturated Fat	1 g
Cholesterol	<1 mg
Sodium	57 mg
Carbohydrate	36 g
Dietary Fiber	3 g
Protein	7 g
Calcium	55 mg
Iron	2 mg
Vitamin A	389 RE
Vitamin C	31 mg

DIETARY EXCHANGES:
2 Starch/Bread, ½ Fruit,
½ Vegetable, ½ Fat

8 ounces uncooked pasta twists
2 cups broccoli florets
⅔ cup shredded carrots
1 medium Red or Golden Delicious apple, cored, seeded and chopped
⅓ cup plain nonfat yogurt
⅓ cup apple juice
3 tablespoons cider vinegar
1 tablespoon light olive oil
1 tablespoon Dijon mustard
1 teaspoon honey
½ teaspoon dried thyme leaves
   Lettuce leaves

1 Cook pasta according to package directions, omitting salt and adding broccoli during the last 2 minutes. Drain and rinse well under cold water until pasta and broccoli are cool; drain well.

2 Place pasta, broccoli, carrots and apple in medium bowl.

3 Combine yogurt, apple juice, cider vinegar, oil, mustard, honey and thyme in small bowl. Pour over pasta mixture; toss to coat evenly.

4 Serve on individual dishes lined with lettuce. Garnish with apple slices, if desired.

Makes 6 (1-cup) servings

SMOKED TURKEY PASTA SALAD

This simple and fast pasta salad can be prepared in advance and refrigerated until you are ready to serve. The smoked turkey gives this salad an imaginative flair.

❖

Nutrients per Serving:

Calories	233
(19% of calories from fat)	
Total Fat	5 g
Saturated Fat	1 g
Cholesterol	12 mg
Sodium	249 mg
Carbohydrate	34 g
Dietary Fiber	5 g
Protein	13 g
Calcium	34 mg
Iron	2 mg
Vitamin A	12 RE
Vitamin C	4 mg

DIETARY EXCHANGES:
2 Starch/Bread, 1 Lean
Meat, ½ Vegetable, ½ Fat

8 ounces uncooked ditalini pasta (small tubes)
6 ounces smoked turkey or chicken breast, skin removed, cut into strips
1 can (15 ounces) light kidney beans, drained and rinsed
½ cup thinly sliced celery
¼ cup chopped red onion
⅓ cup reduced fat mayonnaise
2 tablespoons balsamic vinegar
2 tablespoons chopped fresh chives or green onion
1 tablespoon fresh tarragon *or* 1½ teaspoons dried tarragon leaves
1 teaspoon Dijon mustard
1 clove garlic, minced
¼ teaspoon ground black pepper
Lettuce leaves (optional)

1 Cook pasta according to package directions, omitting salt. Drain and rinse well under cold water until pasta is cool; drain well.

2 Combine pasta with turkey, beans, celery and onion in medium bowl.

3 Combine mayonnaise, vinegar, chives, tarragon, mustard, garlic and pepper in small bowl. Pour over pasta mixture; toss to coat evenly. Serve on lettuce leaves, if desired.

Makes 7 (1-cup) servings

Cook's Tip

❖

Before adding canned beans to a recipe, drain the beans in a colander and rinse thoroughly with fresh cold water. This will wash away much of the sodium as well as some of the complex sugars that sometimes causes flatulence or stomach gas in some people.

❖

GRILLED RATATOUILLE

The uniqueness of this marinated salad lies in the grilling of the vegetables before serving.

Nutrients per Serving:

Calories	115
(18% of calories from fat)	
Total Fat	2 g
Saturated Fat	<1 g
Cholesterol	0 mg
Sodium	91 mg
Carbohydrate	21 g
Dietary Fiber	3 g
Protein	4 g
Calcium	21 mg
Iron	1 mg
Vitamin A	41 RE
Vitamin C	23 mg

DIETARY EXCHANGES:
1 Starch/Bread, ½ Fat,
1 Vegetable

2 points

3 tablespoons red wine vinegar
1 tablespoon olive oil
2 teaspoons fresh thyme
½ teaspoon ground black pepper
4 small Japanese eggplants, cut lengthwise into ½-inch-thick slices
2 small zucchini, cut in half lengthwise
1 medium red onion, quartered
1 red bell pepper, halved and seeded
1 yellow bell pepper, halved and seeded
6 ounces uncooked ziti or penne pasta
½ cup ⅓-less-salt chicken broth
1 tablespoon honey
1 tablespoon Dijon mustard
½ teaspoon Italian seasoning
¼ teaspoon salt
1 cup cherry tomato halves

1 Combine vinegar, oil, thyme and black pepper in shallow bowl. Add eggplants, zucchini, onion and bell peppers; toss to coat evenly. Let stand at room temperature 1 hour or cover and refrigerate overnight.

2 Cook pasta according to package directions, omitting salt. Drain and rinse well under cold water; set aside.

3 Remove vegetables from marinade; reserve marinade. Grill vegetables over medium-hot coals until tender, about 3 to 4 minutes per side. Cool vegetables; cut into 1-inch pieces. Combine vegetables and pasta in large bowl. Add chicken broth, honey, mustard, Italian seasoning and salt to reserved vegetable marinade; whisk to combine. Pour over vegetable-pasta mixture. Gently stir in tomato halves. Serve chilled or at room temperature.   *Makes 9 (1-cup) servings*

HOT CHINESE CHICKEN SALAD

❖

The "hot" in this recipe stands for temperature and level of spice. If the amount of crushed red pepper is too much for you, simply lower the quantity to satisfy your tastebuds.

❖

Nutrients per Serving:

Calories	164
(30% of calories from fat)	
Total Fat	6 g
Saturated Fat	1 g
Cholesterol	45 mg
Sodium	353 mg
Carbohydrate	12 g
Dietary Fiber	2 g
Protein	17 g
Calcium	34 mg
Iron	2 mg
Vitamin A	81 RE
Vitamin C	55 mg

DIETARY EXCHANGES:
½ Starch/Bread, 2 Lean
Meat, 1 Vegetable

4 points

8 ounces fresh or steamed Chinese egg noodles
¼ cup ⅓-less-salt chicken broth
2 tablespoons reduced sodium soy sauce
2 tablespoons rice wine vinegar
1 tablespoon rice wine or dry sherry
1 teaspoon sugar
½ teaspoon crushed red pepper
1 tablespoon vegetable oil, divided
1 clove garlic, minced
1½ cups fresh pea pods, sliced diagonally
1 cup thinly sliced green or red bell pepper
1 pound boneless skinless chicken breasts, cut into ½-inch pieces
1 cup thinly sliced red or green cabbage
2 green onions, thinly sliced

 Cook noodles in boiling water 4 to 5 minutes or until tender. Drain and set aside.

2 Combine chicken broth, soy sauce, vinegar, rice wine, sugar and crushed red pepper in small bowl; set aside.

3 Heat 1 teaspoon oil in large nonstick skillet or wok over high heat. Add garlic, pea pods and bell pepper; cook 1 to 2 minutes or until vegetables are crisp-tender. Set aside.

4 Heat remaining 2 teaspoons oil in skillet. Add chicken and cook 3 to 4 minutes or until chicken is no longer pink. Add cabbage, cooked vegetables and noodles. Stir in sauce; toss to coat evenly. Cook and stir 1 to 2 minutes or until heated through. Sprinkle with green onions before serving.   *Makes 6 (1⅓-cup) servings*

GARBANZO PASTA SALAD

❖

Garbanzo beans can be purchased dried or, for simplicity, canned as they are in this recipe. They are known for their high vegetable protein content.

❖

4 ounces uncooked spinach rotini or fusilli
1 can (15 ounces) garbanzo beans (chickpeas), drained and rinsed
⅓ cup finely chopped carrot
⅓ cup chopped celery
½ cup chopped red bell pepper
2 green onions with tops, chopped
3 tablespoons balsamic vinegar
2 tablespoons reduced calorie mayonnaise
2 teaspoons prepared whole-grain mustard
½ teaspoon ground black pepper
¼ teaspoon Italian seasoning
   Leaf lettuce

1 Cook pasta according to package directions, omitting salt. Drain and rinse well under cold water until pasta is cool; drain well.

2 Combine pasta, garbanzo beans, carrot, celery, bell pepper and green onions in medium bowl.

3 Whisk together vinegar, mayonnaise, mustard, black pepper and Italian seasoning in small bowl until blended. Pour over salad; toss to coat evenly. Cover and refrigerate up to 8 hours.

4 Arrange lettuce on individual plates. Spoon salad over lettuce and garnish with cherry tomatoes, if desired.   *Makes 8 (½-cup) servings*

Nutrients per Serving:	
Calories	129
(16% of calories from fat)	
Total Fat	2 g
Saturated Fat	<1 g
Cholesterol	1 mg
Sodium	242 mg
Carbohydrate	22 g
Dietary Fiber	3 g
Protein	5 g
Calcium	29 mg
Iron	2 mg
Vitamin A	146 RE
Vitamin C	18 mg

DIETARY EXCHANGES:
1½ Starch/Bread, ½ Fat

❖

Health Hint

This recipe makes a wonderful vegetarian main-dish salad. To make optimum use of the vegetable protein in the garbanzo beans, serve this salad with a dairy product.

❖

Soups

VEGETABLE-CHICKEN NOODLE SOUP

If chicken soup is famous for making you feel better, then this soup should keep you feeling great! Loaded with vegetables, this noodle soup is a wonderful start to any meal.

6 cups ⅓-less-salt chicken broth, divided
1 cup chopped celery
½ cup thinly sliced leek (white part only)
½ cup chopped carrot
½ cup peeled and chopped turnip
1 tablespoon minced fresh parsley
1½ teaspoons fresh thyme *or* ½ teaspoon dried thyme leaves
1 teaspoon fresh rosemary *or* ¼ teaspoon dried rosemary
1 teaspoon balsamic vinegar
¼ teaspoon fresh ground black pepper
2 ounces uncooked "no-yolk" broad noodles
1 cup diced cooked chicken

1 Place ⅓ cup chicken broth, celery, leek, carrot and turnip in large saucepan. Cover and cook over medium heat until vegetables are tender, stirring occasionally.

2 Stir in remaining 5⅔ cups chicken broth, parsley, thyme, rosemary, vinegar and black pepper. Bring to a boil; add noodles. Cook until noodles are tender; stir in chicken. Reduce heat to medium. Simmer until heated through.

Makes 6 (1½-cup) servings

Nutrients per Serving:	
Calories	98
(14% of calories from fat)	
Total Fat	2 g
Saturated Fat	<1 g
Cholesterol	18 mg
Sodium	73 mg
Carbohydrate	12 g
Dietary Fiber	1 g
Protein	10 g
Calcium	38 mg
Iron	1 mg
Vitamin A	267 RE
Vitamin C	7 mg

DIETARY EXCHANGES:
½ Starch/Bread, 1 Lean Meat, ½ Vegetable

GREEN CHILE SOUP WITH SPICY BAKED WONTONS

One of the wonders that Christopher Columbus brought from the new world was the mild chili pepper. This enticing recipe comes from the influence of the Szechuan region of China.

❖

Nutrients per Serving:

Calories	150
(24% of calories from fat)	
Total Fat	4 g
Saturated Fat	1 g
Cholesterol	5 mg
Sodium	605 mg
Carbohydrate	32 g
Dietary Fiber	2 g
Protein	5 g
Calcium	199 mg
Iron	2 mg
Vitamin A	159 RE
Vitamin C	44 mg

DIETARY EXCHANGES:
1½ Starch/Bread, ½ Milk,
1 Vegetable, ½ Fat

3 points

½ teaspoon chili powder
⅛ teaspoon garlic powder
⅛ teaspoon onion powder
1 teaspoon water
1 teaspoon vegetable oil
12 fresh or frozen, thawed wonton skins
1 tablespoon reduced calorie margarine
1 leek (white part only) thinly sliced
1 cup chopped celery
2 cloves garlic, minced
½ can (7 ounces) ⅓-less-salt chicken broth
1 cup water
2 cans (4 ounces each) chopped green chilies, drained and rinsed
2 cups skim milk
3 tablespoons all-purpose flour
½ teaspoon ground cumin

1 Preheat oven to 375°F. In small bowl, combine chili powder, garlic powder and onion powder. Stir in 1 teaspoon water and oil.

2 Cut wonton skins in half diagonally and place on large ungreased baking sheet. Brush wontons with chili powder mixture. Bake 5 to 6 minutes or until crisp. Cool completely on wire rack.

3 Heat margarine in medium saucepan over medium-high heat. Add leek, celery and garlic; cook 4 minutes or until softened, stirring occasionally. Stir in chicken broth, 1 cup water and chilies. Heat to a boil.

4 Whisk together milk, flour and cumin until smooth. Add milk mixture to saucepan and cook until thickened, stirring constantly, about 4 minutes.

5 Ladle into individual soup bowls. Serve with wontons. Garnish with fresh cilantro, if desired.

Makes 4 (1-cup) servings

The Japanese udon noodles, called for in this mouth-watering dish, are long, thick wheat noodles with square edges. They are available both fresh and dried.

Nutrients per Serving:

Calories	144
(16% of calories from fat)	
Total Fat	3 g
Saturated Fat	<1 g
Cholesterol	0 mg
Sodium	107 mg
Carbohydrate	24 g
Dietary Fiber	3 g
Protein	9 g
Calcium	56 mg
Iron	3 mg
Vitamin A	374 RE
Vitamin C	16 mg

DIETARY EXCHANGES:
1½ Starch/Bread, ½ Fat,
½ Vegetable

2 - 3 points

JAPANESE NOODLE SOUP

1 package (8½ ounces) Japanese udon noodles
1 teaspoon vegetable oil
1 medium red bell pepper, cut into thin strips
1 medium carrot, diagonally sliced
2 green onions, thinly sliced
2 cans (14½ ounces each) ⅓-less-salt beef broth
1 cup water
1 teaspoon reduced sodium soy sauce
½ teaspoon grated fresh ginger
½ teaspoon ground black pepper
2 cups thinly sliced fresh shiitake mushrooms, stems removed
4 ounces daikon (Japanese radish), peeled and cut into thin strips
4 ounces firm tofu, drained and cut into ½-inch cubes

1 Cook noodles according to package directions, omitting salt. Drain and rinse; set aside.

2 Heat oil in large nonstick saucepan over medium-high heat. Add red bell pepper, carrot and green onions; cook until slightly softened, about 3 minutes. Stir in beef broth, water, soy sauce, ginger and black pepper. Bring to a boil. Add mushrooms, daikon and tofu. Reduce heat and simmer gently 5 minutes or until heated through.

3 Place noodles in soup tureen or individual bowls. Ladle soup over noodles. Serve immediately.

Makes 6 (1½-cup) servings

SPICY LENTIL AND PASTA SOUP

Lentils, a popular meat substitute, have a fair amount of calcium and vitamins A and B, and are a good source of iron and phosphorus.

2 medium onions, thinly sliced
½ cup chopped carrot
½ cup chopped celery
½ cup peeled and chopped turnip
1 small jalapeño pepper, finely chopped
2 cans (14½ ounces each) clear vegetable broth
1 can (14½ ounces) no-salt-added stewed tomatoes
2 cups water
8 ounces dried lentils
2 teaspoons chili powder
½ teaspoon dried oregano
3 ounces uncooked whole wheat spaghetti, broken
¼ cup minced fresh cilantro

1 Spray large nonstick saucepan with nonstick cooking spray. Add onions, carrot, celery, turnip and jalapeño. Cook over medium heat 10 minutes or until vegetables are crisp-tender.

2 Add broth, tomatoes, water, lentils, chili powder and oregano. Bring to a boil. Reduce heat; cover and simmer 20 to 30 minutes or until lentils are tender.

3 Add pasta and cook 10 minutes or until tender.

4 Ladle soup into bowls; sprinkle with cilantro.　　　　*Makes 6 (1¼-cup) servings*

Nutrients per Serving:	
Calories	261
(7% of calories from fat)	
Total Fat	2 g
Saturated Fat	<1 g
Cholesterol	1 mg
Sodium	771 mg
Carbohydrate	49 g
Dietary Fiber	5 g
Protein	15 g
Calcium	65 mg
Iron	6 mg
Vitamin A	475 RE
Vitamin C	27 mg

DIETARY EXCHANGES:
2½ Starch/Bread, ½ Lean Meat, 2 Vegetable

4 points

Cook's Tip
Two ounces of dried long pasta such as spaghetti, is about the same size as the diameter of a quarter.

GINGER WONTON SOUP

❖

A Chinese specialty similar to Italian ravioli, these bite-size dumplings consist of paper-thin dough filled with pork, ricotta cheese, cilantro and Chinese five-spice powder.

❖

Nutrients per Serving:

Calories	259
(17% of calories from fat)	
Total Fat	5 g
Saturated Fat	1 g
Cholesterol	53 mg
Sodium	261 mg
Carbohydrate	39 g
Dietary Fiber	3 g
Protein	16 g
Calcium	74 mg
Iron	3 mg
Vitamin A	72 RE
Vitamin C	43 mg

DIETARY EXCHANGES:
2½ Starch/Bread, 1 Lean Meat, ½ Vegetable, ½ Fat

4 ounces lean ground pork
½ cup reduced fat ricotta cheese
½ tablespoon minced fresh cilantro
½ teaspoon ground black pepper
⅛ teaspoon Chinese five-spice powder
20 fresh or frozen, thawed wonton skins
1 teaspoon vegetable oil
⅓ cup chopped red bell pepper
1 teaspoon grated fresh ginger
2 cans (14½ ounces each) ⅓-less-salt chicken broth
2 teaspoons reduced sodium soy sauce
4 ounces fresh pea pods
1 can (8¾ ounces) baby corn, drained and rinsed
2 green onions, thinly sliced

1 Cook pork in small nonstick skillet over medium-high heat 4 minutes or until no longer pink. Cool slightly; stir in ricotta cheese, cilantro, black pepper and five-spice powder.

2 Place 1 teaspoon filling in center of each wonton skin. Fold top corner of wonton over filling. Lightly brush remaining corners with water. Fold left and right corners over filling. Tightly roll filled end toward remaining corner in jelly-roll fashion. Moisten edges with water to seal. Cover and set aside.

3 Heat oil in large saucepan over medium-high heat. Add bell pepper and ginger; cook 1 minute. Add chicken broth and soy sauce; bring to a boil. Add pea pods, baby corn and wontons. Reduce heat to medium-low and simmer 4 to 5 minutes or until wontons are tender. Sprinkle with green onions.   *Makes 4 (1½-cup) servings*

ENTREES

STRAW AND HAY

1 cup skim milk
½ cup nonfat cottage cheese
2 teaspoons cornstarch
¼ teaspoon ground mace
⅛ teaspoon ground black pepper
4 ounces uncooked fettuccine noodles
4 ounces uncooked spinach fettuccine noodles
4 ounces reduced fat deli-style ham, diagonally sliced
2 tablespoons chopped chives
1 cup frozen peas, thawed and drained
¼ cup grated Parmesan cheese
⅛ teaspoon paprika

1 Combine milk, cottage cheese, cornstarch, mace and black pepper in blender or food processor; process until smooth. Set aside.

2 Cook noodles according to package directions, omitting salt. Drain and set aside.

3 Spray large nonstick skillet with nonstick cooking spray. Cook and stir ham and chives over medium heat until ham is lightly browned. Stir in milk mixture and peas; cook until thickened.

4 Combine noodles and milk mixture in large bowl. Add Parmesan cheese. Toss to coat evenly. Sprinkle with paprika; serve immediately.   *Makes 4 (1½-cup) servings*

Nutrients per Serving:	
Calories	348
(11% of calories from fat)	
Total Fat	4 g
Saturated Fat	2 g
Cholesterol	9 mg
Sodium	592 mg
Carbohydrate	52 g
Dietary Fiber	3 g
Protein	25 g
Calcium	187 mg
Iron	2 mg
Vitamin A	106 RE
Vitamin C	6 mg

DIETARY EXCHANGES:
3 Starch/Bread, 2 Lean
Meat, ½ Fat

7 points

VEGETABLE LASAGNA

Nutrients per Serving:

Calories	273
(21% of calories from fat)	
Total Fat	7 g
Saturated Fat	3 g
Cholesterol	19 mg
Sodium	424 mg
Carbohydrate	37 g
Dietary Fiber	6 g
Protein	21 g
Calcium	409 mg
Iron	4 mg
Vitamin A	918 RE
Vitamin C	75 mg

DIETARY EXCHANGES:
1 Starch/Bread, 2 Lean
Meat, 4 Vegetable

Tomato Sauce (page 118)
8 ounces uncooked lasagna noodles (9 noodles)
2 teaspoons olive oil
⅓ cup finely chopped carrot
2 cloves garlic, minced
2 cups coarsely chopped fresh mushrooms
3 cups coarsely chopped broccoli, including stems
1 package (10 ounces) frozen chopped spinach, thawed and drained
⅛ teaspoon ground nutmeg
1 container (15 ounces) nonfat ricotta cheese
2 tablespoons minced fresh parsley
1 tablespoon minced fresh basil
1 tablespoon minced fresh oregano
2 teaspoons cornstarch
¼ teaspoon ground black pepper
1½ cups (6 ounces) shredded part-skim mozzarella cheese, divided
2 tablespoons grated Parmesan cheese

1 Prepare Tomato Sauce. Set aside. Cook noodles according to package directions, omitting salt. Drain and rinse well under cold water. Place noodles on sheet of aluminum foil.

2 Heat olive oil in large nonstick skillet over medium heat. Add carrot and garlic; cook until garlic is soft, about 3 minutes. Add mushrooms; cook and stir until moisture is evaporated. Reduce heat. Add broccoli; cover and simmer 3 to 5 minutes or until broccoli is crisp-tender. Remove from heat; stir in spinach and nutmeg.

3 Preheat oven to 350°F. Combine ricotta cheese, parsley, basil, oregano, cornstarch and black pepper in small bowl. Stir in 1¼ cups mozzarella cheese.

4 Lightly spray 13×9-inch baking dish with nonstick cooking spray. Spread 2 tablespoons Tomato Sauce in bottom of dish. Arrange 3 noodles in dish. Spread with ½ cheese mixture and ½ vegetable mixture. Pour ⅓ tomato sauce over vegetable layer. Repeat layers, ending with noodles. Pour remaining ⅓ tomato sauce over noodles. Sprinkle with Parmesan cheese and remaining ¼ cup mozzarella. Cover; bake 30 minutes. Uncover; continue baking 10 to 15 minutes or until bubbly and heated through. Let stand 10 minutes. *Makes 10 servings*

(continued on page 118)

Vegetable Lasagna, continued

TOMATO SAUCE

    2 cans (16 ounces each) whole, peeled tomatoes, undrained
    2 cans (6 ounces each) no-salt-added tomato paste
    1 medium onion, finely chopped
    ¼ cup red wine
    2 cloves garlic, minced
    1 tablespoon Italian seasoning

1 Combine tomatoes, tomato paste, onion, red wine, garlic and Italian seasoning in medium saucepan. Cover. Bring to a boil; reduce heat. Simmer 20 minutes.

❖

Health Hint

Tomatoes are an excellent source of antioxidants. Studies suggest that antioxidants may reduce the risk of some forms of cancer, heart disease, strokes, as well as slow the aging process.

❖

KOREAN-STYLE BEEF AND PASTA

❖

Rice noodles, also known as rice sticks, are made from rice flour and are as thin as string. They are usually coiled into nests and packaged in plastic bags.

❖

Nutrients per Serving:

Calories	194
(19% of calories from fat)	
Total Fat	4 g
Saturated Fat	1 g
Cholesterol	29 mg
Sodium	668 mg
Carbohydrate	24 g
Dietary Fiber	1 g
Protein	13 g
Calcium	37 mg
Iron	3 mg
Vitamin A	309 RE
Vitamin C	37 mg

DIETARY EXCHANGES:
1½ Starch/Bread, 1½ Lean
Meat, ½ Vegetable

4 points

¾ pound lean round steak
2 tablespoons reduced sodium soy sauce
1 tablespoon rice wine
2 teaspoons sugar
   Korean-Style Dressing (page 120)
1 package (6¾ ounces) rice noodles
2 cups thinly sliced napa cabbage
1¾ cups thinly sliced yellow bell peppers
½ cup thinly sliced radishes
1 medium carrot, shredded
2 green onions, thinly sliced

1 Freeze beef until partially firm; cut into very thin slices.

2 Combine soy sauce, rice wine and sugar in small nonmetallic bowl. Add beef slices; toss to coat evenly. Cover and refrigerate 8 hours or overnight.

3 Drain beef; grill over medium-hot coals 2 to 3 minutes or until desired doneness.

4 Meanwhile, prepare Korean-Style Dressing; set aside.

5 Cook noodles in boiling water 1 to 2 minutes or until tender; drain and rinse under cold water. Arrange noodles on platter.

6 Combine cabbage, bell peppers, radishes, carrot, green onions and beef in medium bowl. Add Korean-Style Dressing; toss to coat evenly. Serve over noodles. Garnish with green onion brush and carrot ribbons, if desired.   *Makes 8 (1-cup) servings*

(continued on page 120)

Korean-Style Beef and Pasta, continued

KOREAN-STYLE DRESSING

    2 teaspoons sesame seeds
    ⅓ cup orange juice
    2 tablespoons rice wine
    2 teaspoons reduced sodium soy sauce
    1 teaspoon Oriental sesame oil
    1 teaspoon grated fresh ginger
    1 teaspoon sugar
    1 clove garlic, minced
    ⅛ teaspoon crushed red pepper

1 Place sesame seeds in small nonstick skillet. Cook and stir over medium heat until lightly browned and toasted, about 5 minutes. Cool completely.

2 Crush sesame seeds using mortar and pestle or with wooden spoon; transfer to small bowl.

3 Add orange juice, rice wine, soy sauce, sesame oil, ginger, sugar, garlic and crushed red pepper to sesame seeds. Blend well.

❖

Cook's Tip
When peeling fresh ginger, be careful to remove only the skin because the flesh just under the surface is the most flavorful part.

❖

CHEESE TORTELLINI WITH TUNA

❖

*Cheese tortellini and tuna
both provide good sources of
protein. Add a green salad to
complete this delicious meal.*

❖

Nutrients per Serving:

Calories	180
(19% of calories from fat)	
Total Fat	4 g
Saturated Fat	2 g
Cholesterol	21 mg
Sodium	160 mg
Carbohydrate	21 g
Dietary Fiber	3 g
Protein	16 g
Calcium	141 mg
Iron	2 mg
Vitamin A	397 RE
Vitamin C	112 mg

DIETARY EXCHANGES:
½ Starch/Bread, 1½ Lean
Meat, ½ Milk, 1 Vegetable

1 tuna steak* (about 6 ounces)
1 package (9 ounces) reduced fat cheese tortellini
1 cup finely chopped red bell pepper
1 cup finely chopped green bell pepper
¼ cup finely chopped onion
¾ teaspoon fennel seeds, crushed
½ cup evaporated skim milk
2 teaspoons all-purpose flour
½ teaspoon dry mustard
½ teaspoon ground black pepper

1 Grill or broil tuna 4 inches from heat source until fish just begins to flake, about 7 to 9 minutes. Remove and discard skin. Cut tuna into chunks; set aside.

2 Cook pasta according to package directions, omitting salt. Drain; set aside.

3 Spray large nonstick skillet with nonstick cooking spray. Add bell peppers, onion and fennel seeds; cook over medium heat until crisp-tender.

4 Whisk together milk, flour, mustard and black pepper in small bowl until smooth; add to skillet. Cook until thickened, stirring constantly. Stir in tuna and pasta; reduce heat and simmer until heated through, about 3 minutes. Serve immediately.

Makes about 4 (1½-cup) servings

*Or, substitute 1 can (6 ounces) tuna packed in water, drained, for tuna steak.

PAD THAI

❖

This lighter version of the traditional Thai dish is an excellent choice when you're in the mood for something just a little different.

❖

Nutrients per Serving:

Calories	265
(18% of calories from fat)	
Total Fat	6 g
Saturated Fat	1 g
Cholesterol	38 mg
Sodium	798 mg
Carbohydrate	42 g
Dietary Fiber	1 g
Protein	14 g
Calcium	78 mg
Iron	2 mg
Vitamin A	453 RE
Vitamin C	13 mg

DIETARY EXCHANGES:
2½ Starch/Bread, ½ Lean
Meat, 1 Vegetable, ½ Fat

8 ounces uncooked rice noodles, ⅛ inch wide
1½ tablespoons fish sauce*
1 to 2 tablespoons fresh lemon juice
2 tablespoons rice wine vinegar
1 tablespoon ketchup
2 teaspoons sugar
¼ teaspoon crushed red pepper
1 tablespoon vegetable oil
4 ounces boneless skinless chicken breast, finely chopped
2 green onions, thinly sliced
2 cloves garlic, minced
3 ounces raw small shrimp, peeled and deveined
2 cups fresh bean sprouts
1 medium carrot, shredded
3 tablespoons minced fresh cilantro
2 tablespoons chopped unsalted dry-roasted peanuts

1 Place noodles in medium bowl. Cover with lukewarm water and let stand 30 minutes or until soft. Drain and set aside. Whisk together fish sauce, lemon juice, rice wine vinegar, ketchup, sugar and crushed red pepper in small bowl; set aside.

2 Heat oil in wok or large nonstick skillet over medium-high heat. Add chicken, green onions and garlic. Cook and stir until chicken is no longer pink. Stir in noodles; cook 1 minute. Add shrimp and bean sprouts; cook just until shrimp turn opaque, about 3 minutes. Stir in fish sauce mixture; toss to coat evenly. Cook until heated through, about 2 minutes.

3 Arrange noodle mixture on platter; sprinkle with carrot, cilantro and peanuts. Garnish with lemon wedges, tomato wedges and fresh cilantro, if desired.

Makes 5 (1-cup) servings

*Fish sauce is available at most larger supermarkets and Oriental markets.

EASY TEX-MEX BAKE

❖

*Tex-Mex is quickly becoming
one of the most requested
flavor combinations. If that
is the taste you're looking
for, you won't be
disappointed with this
low fat dish.*

❖

Nutrients per Serving:

Calories	365
(15% of calories from fat)	
Total Fat	6 g
Saturated Fat	3 g
Cholesterol	99 mg
Sodium	800 mg
Carbohydrate	39 g
Dietary Fiber	4 g
Protein	38 g
Calcium	147 mg
Iron	3 mg
Vitamin A	166 RE
Vitamin C	26 mg

DIETARY EXCHANGES:
2 Starch/Bread, 4 Lean
Meat

7 points

8 ounces uncooked thin mostaccioli
1 pound ground turkey breast
1 package (10 ounces) frozen corn, thawed, drained
⅔ cup bottled medium or mild salsa
1 container (16 ounces) low fat cottage cheese
1 egg
1 tablespoon minced fresh cilantro
½ teaspoon ground white pepper
¼ teaspoon ground cumin
½ cup (2 ounces) shredded Monterey Jack cheese

1 Cook pasta according to package directions, omitting salt. Drain and rinse well; set aside.

2 Spray large nonstick skillet with nonstick cooking spray. Add turkey; cook over high heat until no longer pink, about 5 minutes. Stir in corn and salsa. Remove from heat.

3 Preheat oven to 350°F. Combine cottage cheese, egg, cilantro, white pepper and cumin in small bowl.

4 Spoon ½ turkey mixture in bottom of 11½×7½-inch baking dish. Top with pasta. Spoon cottage cheese mixture over pasta. Top with remaining turkey mixture. Sprinkle Monterey Jack cheese over casserole.

5 Bake 25 to 30 minutes or until heated through.   *Makes 6 servings*

PASTA PRIMAVERA

In Italian, primavera means "spring style." By including so many fresh vegetables, this famous entrée has been referred to as a "garden on a plate."

Nutrients per Serving:

Calories	329
(16% of calories from fat)	
Total Fat	6 g
Saturated Fat	2 g
Cholesterol	8 mg
Sodium	243 mg
Carbohydrate	51 g
Dietary Fiber	6 g
Protein	18 g
Calcium	265 mg
Iron	4 mg
Vitamin A	167 RE
Vitamin C	82 mg

DIETARY EXCHANGES:
2½ Starch/Bread, ½ Lean
Meat, 1½ Vegetable,
½ Milk

8 ounces uncooked linguine or medium pasta shells
1 tablespoon reduced calorie margarine
2 green onions, diagonally sliced
1 clove garlic, minced
1 cup fresh mushroom slices
1 cup broccoli florets
2½ cups fresh snow peas
4 to 8 asparagus spears, cut into 2-inch pieces
1 medium red bell pepper, cut into thin strips
½ cup evaporated skimmed milk
½ teaspoon dried tarragon leaves
½ teaspoon ground black pepper
⅓ cup grated Parmesan cheese

1 Cook pasta according to package directions, omitting salt. Drain and set aside.

2 Melt margarine in large nonstick skillet over medium-high heat. Add green onions and garlic; cook until softened. Add mushrooms and broccoli. Cover. Cook 3 minutes or until mushrooms are tender.

3 Add snow peas, asparagus, bell pepper, milk, tarragon and black pepper. Cook and stir until vegetables are crisp-tender and lightly coated.

4 Add cheese; toss to coat evenly. Serve immediately.   *Makes 4 (2-cup) servings*

FAJITA STUFFED SHELLS

❖

*Mexican and Italian meet in
this enticing entrée.
Flavored with lime, garlic,
oregano, cumin and
cilantro, it tastes much more
complicated than it is.*

❖

Nutrients per Serving:

Calories	265
(16% of calories from fat)	
Total Fat	5 g
Saturated Fat	2 g
Cholesterol	33 mg
Sodium	341 mg
Carbohydrate	36 g
Dietary Fiber	3 g
Protein	19 g
Calcium	98 mg
Iron	3 mg
Vitamin A	99 RE
Vitamin C	38 mg

DIETARY EXCHANGES:
2 Starch/Bread, 1½ Lean
Meat, 1 Vegetable

5 points

¼ cup fresh lime juice
1 clove garlic, minced
½ teaspoon dried oregano leaves
¼ teaspoon ground cumin
1 (6-ounce) boneless lean round or flank steak
1 medium green bell pepper, halved and seeded
1 medium onion, cut in half
12 uncooked jumbo pasta shells (about 6 ounces)
½ cup reduced fat sour cream
2 tablespoons shredded reduced fat Cheddar cheese
1 tablespoon minced fresh cilantro
⅔ cup bottled chunky salsa
2 cups shredded leaf lettuce

1 Combine lime juice, garlic, oregano and cumin in shallow nonmetallic dish. Add steak, bell pepper and onion. Cover and refrigerate 8 hours or overnight.

2 Preheat oven to 350°F. Cook pasta shells according to package directions, omitting salt. Drain and rinse well under cold water; set aside.

3 Grill steak and vegetables over medium-hot coals 3 to 4 minutes per side or until desired doneness; cool slightly. Cut steak into thin slices. Chop vegetables. Place steak slices and vegetables in medium bowl. Stir in sour cream, Cheddar cheese and cilantro. Stuff shells evenly with meat mixture, mounding slightly.

4 Arrange shells in 8-inch baking dish. Pour salsa over filled shells. Cover with foil and bake 15 minutes or until heated through. Divide lettuce evenly among 4 plates; arrange 3 shells on each plate.

Makes 4 servings

JAMBALAYA

In Italian, orzo means "barley," but it is actually a tiny, rice-shaped pasta. It is ideal for soups and wonderful when served as a substitute for rice, as it is in this spicy dish.

❖

Nutrients per Serving:

Calories	359
(11% of calories from fat)	
Total Fat	5 g
Saturated Fat	1 g
Cholesterol	24 mg
Sodium	728 mg
Carbohydrate	62 g
Dietary Fiber	11 g
Protein	20 g
Calcium	113 mg
Iron	5 mg
Vitamin A	156 RE
Vitamin C	102 mg

DIETARY EXCHANGES:
3 Starch/Bread, 1 Lean
Meat, 3 Vegetable

6 points

2 teaspoons vegetable oil
4 ounces smoked chicken, cubed
1½ cups chopped green bell pepper
1¼ cups chopped celery
1 cup chopped onion
3 cloves garlic, minced
1 can (16 ounces) no-salt-added tomatoes, undrained and cut up
2 bay leaves
½ teaspoon dried thyme leaves
¼ teaspoon dry mustard
¼ teaspoon ground black pepper
3 to 5 dashes hot pepper sauce
1 cup uncooked orzo pasta
1 can (15.5 ounces) red kidney beans, drained and rinsed
¼ cup thinly sliced green onions

1 Heat oil in large nonstick saucepan over medium-high heat. Add chicken and cook until lightly browned, about 2 minutes. Add bell pepper, celery, onion and garlic. Cook, stirring frequently, 5 minutes or until vegetables are tender.

2 Add tomatoes, bay leaves, thyme, mustard, black pepper and hot pepper sauce. Bring to a boil; reduce heat and simmer 10 minutes or until slightly thickened. Remove bay leaves.

3 Cook pasta according to package directions, omitting salt. Drain, but do not rinse.

4 Stir beans into tomato mixture. Cook 5 minutes or until heated through.

5 Spoon approximately ½ cup pasta into individual bowls. Spoon jambalaya over pasta. Sprinkle with green onions. Garnish as desired.

Makes 4 servings

CHICKEN CHOW MEIN

Chow Mein is a Chinese-American dish consisting of bits of meat and vegetables traditionally served over crispy fried noodles. This lighter version eliminates the extra fat and calories by baking the noodles instead.

❖

Nutrients per Serving:	
Calories	284
(6% of calories from fat)	
Total Fat	2 g
Saturated Fat	<1 g
Cholesterol	22 mg
Sodium	322 mg
Carbohydrate	52 g
Dietary Fiber	3 g
Protein	16 g
Calcium	57 mg
Iron	3 mg
Vitamin A	350 RE
Vitamin C	23 mg

DIETARY EXCHANGES:
2 Starch/Bread, 1 Lean
Meat, 3 Vegetable

5 points

6 ounces uncooked fresh Chinese egg noodles
    Nonstick cooking spray
½ cup ⅓-less-salt chicken broth
2 tablespoons reduced sodium soy sauce
1½ teaspoons cornstarch
½ teaspoon Oriental sesame oil
½ teaspoon ground black pepper
⅛ teaspoon Chinese five-spice powder
6 ounces boneless skinless chicken breasts, coarsely chopped
2 green onions, sliced
2 cups thinly sliced bok choy
1½ cups mixed frozen vegetables, thawed and drained
1 can (8 ounces) sliced water chestnuts, drained and rinsed
1 cup fresh bean sprouts

1 Preheat oven to 400°F. Cook noodles according to package directions, omitting salt. Drain and rinse well under cold water until pasta is cool; drain well. Lightly spray 9-inch cake pan with nonstick cooking spray. Spread noodles in pan, pressing firmly. Lightly spray top of noodles with nonstick cooking spray. Bake 10 minutes.

2 Invert noodles onto baking sheet or large plate. Carefully slide noodle cake back into cake pan. Bake 10 to 15 minutes or until top is crisp and lightly browned. Transfer to serving platter. Whisk together chicken broth, soy sauce, cornstarch, sesame oil, black pepper and five-spice powder in small bowl until cornstarch is dissolved; set aside.

3 Spray large nonstick skillet with nonstick cooking spray. Add chicken and green onions. Cook over medium-high heat, stirring frequently, until chicken is no longer pink, about 5 minutes. Stir in bok choy, mixed vegetables and water chestnuts. Cook 3 minutes or until vegetables are crisp-tender. Push vegetables to one side of skillet; stir in sauce. Cook and stir until thickened, about 2 minutes. Stir in bean sprouts. Spoon over noodle cake.

Makes 4 servings

DOUBLE SPINACH BAKE

Cooked spinach explodes with vitamin A and beta-carotene! This entrée packs a double punch by using spinach fettuccine.

8 ounces uncooked spinach fettuccine noodles
1 cup fresh mushroom slices
1 green onion with top, finely chopped
1 clove garlic, minced
4 to 5 cups fresh spinach, coarsely chopped *or* 1 package (10 ounces) frozen spinach, thawed and drained
1 tablespoon water
1 container (15 ounces) nonfat ricotta cheese
¼ cup skim milk
1 egg
½ teaspoon ground nutmeg
½ teaspoon ground black pepper
¼ cup (1 ounce) shredded reduced fat Swiss cheese

1 Preheat oven to 350°F. Cook pasta according to package directions, omitting salt. Drain; set aside.

2 Spray medium skillet with nonstick cooking spray. Add mushrooms, green onion and garlic. Cook and stir over medium heat until mushrooms are softened. Add spinach and water. Cover; cook until spinach is wilted, about 3 minutes.

3 Combine ricotta cheese, milk, egg, nutmeg and black pepper in large bowl. Gently stir in noodles and vegetables; toss to coat evenly.

4 Lightly coat shallow 1½-quart casserole with nonstick cooking spray. Spread noodle mixture in casserole. Sprinkle with Swiss cheese.

5 Bake 25 to 30 minutes or until knife inserted halfway to center comes out clean.

Makes 6 (1-cup) servings

Nutrients per Serving:

Calories	235
(9% of calories from fat)	
Total Fat	3 g
Saturated Fat	<1 g
Cholesterol	46 mg
Sodium	110 mg
Carbohydrate	41 g
Dietary Fiber	1 g
Protein	19 g
Calcium	57 mg
Iron	1 mg
Vitamin A	280 RE
Vitamin C	12 mg

DIETARY EXCHANGES:
2 Starch/Bread, 1½ Lean Meat, ½ Vegetable

5 points

ENLIGHTENED MACARONI AND CHEESE

This twist on an all-time American favorite is guaranteed to make your family smile, and it's low in fat too!

❖

Nutrients per Serving:	
Calories	266
(19% of calories from fat)	
Total Fat	6 g
Saturated Fat	3 g
Cholesterol	18 mg
Sodium	200 mg
Carbohydrate	35 g
Dietary Fiber	2 g
Protein	18 g
Calcium	406 mg
Iron	2 mg
Vitamin A	125 RE
Vitamin C	11 mg

DIETARY EXCHANGES:
2 Starch/Bread, 1 Lean
Meat, ½ Milk, ½ Fat

5 points

8 ounces uncooked wagon wheel, bow tie or elbow pasta
1 tablespoon all-purpose flour
2 teaspoons cornstarch
¼ teaspoon dry mustard
1 can (12 ounces) evaporated skimmed milk
1 cup (4 ounces) shredded reduced fat medium sharp Cheddar cheese
½ cup (2 ounces) shredded reduced fat Monterey Jack cheese
1 jar (2 ounces) diced pimiento, drained and rinsed
1 teaspoon Worcestershire sauce
¼ teaspoon ground black pepper
1 tablespoon dry bread crumbs
1 tablespoon paprika

1 Preheat oven to 375°F.

2 Cook pasta according to package directions, omitting salt. Drain and set aside.

3 Combine flour, cornstarch and mustard in medium saucepan; stir in milk until smooth. Cook over low heat, stirring occasionally, until slightly thickened, about 8 minutes.

4 Remove from heat; stir in cheeses, pimiento, Worcestershire sauce and black pepper. Add pasta; mix well.

5 Spray 1½-quart casserole with nonstick cooking spray. Spoon mixture into casserole; sprinkle with bread crumbs and paprika.

6 Bake 20 minutes or until bubbly and heated through.   *Makes 6 (1-cup) servings*

CHICKEN NOODLE ROLL-UPS

Serve this colorful lasagna-like dish for a special occasion!

❖

Nutrients per Serving:	
Calories	179
(22% of calories from fat)	
Total Fat	4 g
Saturated Fat	1 g
Cholesterol	46 mg
Sodium	291 mg
Carbohydrate	17 g
Dietary Fiber	2 g
Protein	18 g
Calcium	77 mg
Iron	1 mg
Vitamin A	95 RE
Vitamin C	24 mg

DIETARY EXCHANGES:
1 Starch/Bread, 2 Lean
Meat

3 - 4 points

2 strips = 7 pts

9 uncooked lasagna noodles (about 9 ounces)
8 ounces boneless skinless chicken breasts, cut into chunks
2 cups finely chopped broccoli
2 cups low fat cottage cheese
1 egg
2 teaspoons minced fresh chives
¼ teaspoon ground nutmeg
¼ teaspoon ground black pepper
1 tablespoon reduced calorie margarine
2 tablespoons all-purpose flour
1 cup ⅓-less-salt chicken broth
½ cup skim milk
½ teaspoon dry mustard
1 medium tomato, seeded and chopped

1 Cook lasagna noodles according to package directions, omitting salt. Drain and rinse well under cold water. Place in single layer on aluminum foil.

2 Preheat oven to 375°F. Place chicken in food processor or blender; process until finely chopped. Spray large nonstick skillet with nonstick cooking spray; place over medium heat. Add chicken; cook 4 minutes or until chicken is no longer pink. Stir in broccoli; cook until broccoli is crisp-tender, about 3 minutes. Cool.

3 Combine cottage cheese, egg, chives, nutmeg and black pepper in medium bowl. Stir in chicken mixture. Spread generous ⅓ cup filling over each lasagna noodle. Roll up noodles, starting at short end. Place filled rolls, seam side down, in 10×8-inch baking dish; set aside.

4 Melt margarine in small saucepan over medium-high heat. Stir in flour; cook 1 minute. Whisk in chicken broth, milk and mustard. Cook, stirring constantly, until thickened. Pour sauce over filled rolls; sprinkle with tomato. Cover dish with foil. Bake 30 to 35 minutes or until filling is set.   *Makes 9 servings*

ORANGE BEEF AND BROCCOLI

Broccoli is said to be one of the healthiest foods you can eat! It is loaded with antioxidants and cancer-fighting agents, such as vitamin C.

❖

Nutrients per Serving:

Calories	424
(27% of calories from fat)	
Total Fat	13 g
Saturated Fat	3 g
Cholesterol	77 mg
Sodium	169 mg
Carbohydrate	43 g
Dietary Fiber	6 g
Protein	35 g
Calcium	69 mg
Iron	5 mg
Vitamin A	943 RE
Vitamin C	125 mg

DIETARY EXCHANGES:
2 Starch/Bread, 3½ Lean
Meat, 2½ Vegetable,
½ Fat

1 pound lean boneless sirloin, cut 1 inch thick
½ cup orange juice
2 teaspoons reduced sodium soy sauce
1 teaspoon sugar
3 teaspoons vegetable oil, divided
¾ pound broccoli, coarsely chopped
1 cup diagonally sliced carrots
½ cup thinly sliced red bell pepper
1 green onion, diagonally sliced
2 teaspoons cornstarch
¾ cup cold water
1 tablespoon grated orange peel
6 ounces uncooked "no-yolk" broad noodles

1 Slice beef across grain into ⅛-inch-thick slices. Place beef strips in medium glass or nonmetallic bowl. Add orange juice, soy sauce and sugar; toss to coat evenly. Let stand 30 minutes, or cover and refrigerate overnight.

2 Heat 2 teaspoons oil in large nonstick skillet or wok over high heat. Add broccoli, carrots, bell pepper and green onion. Cook 2 minutes, stirring frequently. Remove vegetables to large bowl.

3 Heat remaining 1 teaspoon oil in skillet. Drain beef strips; reserve marinade. Add beef to skillet; cook 1 to 2 minutes or until no longer pink. Add vegetables and reserved marinade to skillet. Bring to a boil. Stir cornstarch into water until smooth. Add to skillet and cook until thickened, stirring constantly. Sprinkle with grated orange peel.

4 Cook noodles according to package directions, omitting salt. Drain. Spoon beef mixture over noodles and serve immediately. Garnish with orange curls, if desired.

Makes 4 servings

SANTA FE FUSILLI

❖

When you have a taste for something hearty and healthy, this full-flavored Texas-style dish is for you!

❖

Nutrients per Serving:

Calories	228
(9% of calories from fat)	
Total Fat	2 g
Saturated Fat	<1 g
Cholesterol	3 mg
Sodium	215 mg
Carbohydrate	46 g
Dietary Fiber	8 g
Protein	12 g
Calcium	41 mg
Iron	2 mg
Vitamin A	189 RE
Vitamin C	57 mg

DIETARY EXCHANGES:
2 Starch/Bread, ½ Lean
Meat, 2½ Vegetable

3 points

1 medium red bell pepper*
2 teaspoons cumin seeds
¾ cup chopped, seeded tomato
¼ cup chopped onion
1 clove garlic, minced
1 tablespoon chili powder
¼ teaspoon crushed red pepper
¼ teaspoon ground black pepper
1 can (16 ounces) no-salt-added tomato purée
⅓ cup water
1 teaspoon sugar
8 ounces uncooked fusilli pasta
1 can (16 ounces) black beans, drained and rinsed
1 package (10 ounces) frozen corn, thawed and drained
1 can (4 ounces) chopped green chilies, drained
⅓ cup low fat sour cream
   Fresh cilantro

1 Roast bell pepper over charcoal or gas flame or place under broiler, turning several times, until skin is charred. Cool 10 minutes. Peel and discard charred skin. Cut pepper in half; seed and coarsely chop.

2 Place cumin seeds in large nonstick saucepan. Cook and stir over medium heat until lightly toasted, about 3 minutes. Stir in tomato, onion, garlic, chili powder, crushed red pepper and black pepper. Cook until vegetables are tender, about 5 minutes. Stir in tomato purée, water and sugar. Reduce heat to low. Cover and simmer 15 minutes.

3 Cook pasta according to package directions, omitting salt. Drain and set aside. Stir in beans, corn and chilies into vegetable mixture. Cook until heated through, about 8 minutes. Stir in pasta. Spoon into individual bowls; top with sour cream and cilantro.

Makes 8 (1-cup) servings

*Or, substitute 1 jar (7 ounces) roasted peppers, drained and chopped and omit step 1.

PASTITSO

❖

Replacing real eggs with egg substitute in this fabulous Greek dish significantly reduces the amount of cholesterol normally found here.

❖

Nutrients per Serving:

Calories	280
(15% of calories from fat)	
Total Fat	5 g
Saturated Fat	2 g
Cholesterol	31 mg
Sodium	366 mg
Carbohydrate	39 g
Dietary Fiber	1 g
Protein	20 g
Calcium	134 mg
Iron	3 mg
Vitamin A	198 RE
Vitamin C	4 mg

DIETARY EXCHANGES:
2½ Starch/Bread, 1½ Lean
Meat, ½ Vegetable

6 points

    8 ounces uncooked elbow macaroni
  ½ cup cholesterol free egg substitute
  ¼ teaspoon ground nutmeg
  ¾ pound lean ground lamb, beef or turkey
  ½ cup chopped onion
    1 clove garlic, minced
    1 can (8 ounces) tomato sauce
  ¾ teaspoon dried mint leaves
  ½ teaspoon dried oregano leaves
  ½ teaspoon ground black pepper
  ⅛ teaspoon ground cinnamon
    2 teaspoons reduced calorie margarine
    3 tablespoons all-purpose flour
1½ cups skim milk
    2 tablespoons grated Parmesan cheese

1 Cook pasta according to package directions, omitting salt. Drain and transfer to medium bowl; stir in egg substitute and nutmeg.

2 Lightly spray bottom of 9-inch square baking dish with nonstick cooking spray. Spread pasta mixture in bottom of baking dish. Set aside.

3 Preheat oven to 350°F. Cook lamb, onion and garlic in large nonstick skillet over medium heat until lamb is no longer pink. Stir in tomato sauce, mint, oregano, black pepper and cinnamon. Reduce heat and simmer 10 minutes; spread over pasta.

4 Melt margarine in small nonstick saucepan over medium-high heat. Add flour. Stir constantly for 1 minute. Whisk in milk. Cook, stirring constantly, until thickened, about 6 minutes; spread over meat mixture. Sprinkle with Parmesan cheese. Bake 30 to 40 minutes or until set.

Makes 6 servings

THAI BEEF NOODLES

Today more than ever, lean beef can be included in heart-healthy diets. This fabulous dish incorporates many traditional Thai ingredients—without all the fat.

Nutrients per Serving:

Calories	400
(29% of calories from fat)	
Total Fat	13 g
Saturated Fat	4 g
Cholesterol	76 mg
Sodium	790 mg
Carbohydrate	40 g
Dietary Fiber	1 g
Protein	33 g
Calcium	35 mg
Iron	5 mg
Vitamin A	48 RE
Vitamin C	52 mg

DIETARY EXCHANGES:
2½ Starch/Bread, 3½ Lean Meat, 1 Vegetable, ½ Fat

1 pound lean boneless top sirloin, cut 1 inch thick
2 tablespoons reduced sodium soy sauce, divided
2 tablespoons rice wine or dry sherry
2 teaspoons sugar
2 tablespoons water
1 tablespoon creamy peanut butter
2 teaspoons rice wine vinegar
¼ teaspoon crushed red pepper
⅛ teaspoon grated fresh ginger
6 ounces uncooked vermicelli or other pasta
1 cup chopped red bell pepper
¾ cup chopped, seeded cucumber
¼ cup diagonally sliced green onions

1 Cut steak into 1-inch pieces; place in medium glass or nonmetallic bowl. Add 1 tablespoon soy sauce, rice wine and sugar to beef; toss to coat evenly. Let stand 30 minutes, or cover and refrigerate overnight.

2 Combine remaining 1 tablespoon soy sauce, water, peanut butter, rice wine vinegar, crushed red pepper and ginger in large bowl.

3 Cook pasta according to package directions, omitting salt. Drain and rinse well under hot water. Add pasta to peanut butter mixture; toss to coat evenly. Set aside. Drain beef; discard marinade.

4 Spray large nonstick skillet with nonstick cooking spray; heat over medium-high heat. Add beef and bell pepper to skillet. Cook 2 to 3 minutes or until desired doneness. Add beef and bell pepper to pasta mixture; toss to coat evenly. Sprinkle with cucumber and green onions.   *Makes 4 servings*

SIDE DISHES

LEMON TOSSED LINGUINE

Lemon is rapidly becoming an appealing substitute for high fat sauces. Once you've tried this exceptional combination, you may never go back to your original sauces.

8 ounces uncooked linguine noodles
3 tablespoons fresh lemon juice
2 teaspoons reduced calorie margarine
2 tablespoons minced chives
⅓ cup skim milk
1 teaspoon cornstarch
1 tablespoon minced fresh dill *or* 1 teaspoon dried dill weed
1 tablespoon minced fresh parsley *or* 1 teaspoon dried parsley
2 teaspoons grated lemon peel
¼ teaspoon ground white pepper
3 tablespoons grated Romano or Parmesan cheese

1 Cook noodles according to package directions, omitting salt. Drain well. Place in medium bowl; pour lemon juice over noodles.

2 Meanwhile, melt margarine in small saucepan over medium heat. Add chives and cook until chives are soft. Combine milk and cornstarch; stir into saucepan. Cook and stir until thickened. Stir in dill, parsley, lemon peel and white pepper.

3 Pour milk mixture over noodles. Sprinkle with cheese; toss to coat evenly. Garnish with lemon slices and dill sprigs, if desired. Serve immediately.

Makes 6 (½-cup) servings

Nutrients per Serving:	
Calories	173
(18% of calories from fat)	
Total Fat	3 g
Saturated Fat	1 g
Cholesterol	7 mg
Sodium	110 mg
Carbohydrate	27 g
Dietary Fiber	2 g
Protein	8 g
Calcium	104 mg
Iron	1 mg
Vitamin A	51 RE
Vitamin C	6 mg

DIETARY EXCHANGES:
1½ Starch/Bread, ½ Lean Meat, ½ Fat

TOASTED SESAME ORZO

❖

*Iron, found in spinach, is
needed by the body to aid in
the proper function of the
immune system and in the
production of connective
tissue.*

❖

Nutrients per Serving:

Calories	116
(19% of calories from fat)	
Total Fat	2 g
Saturated Fat	1 g
Cholesterol	2 mg
Sodium	72 mg
Carbohydrate	19 g
Dietary Fiber	1 g
Protein	5 g
Calcium	68 mg
Iron	1 mg
Vitamin A	110 RE
Vitamin C	4 mg

DIETARY EXCHANGES:
1 Starch/Bread, ½ Fat,
1 Vegetable

2 points

1 tablespoon sesame seeds
⅔ cup uncooked orzo pasta
1 teaspoon reduced calorie margarine
1½ cups fresh spinach, washed and coarsely chopped
1 clove garlic, minced
3 tablespoons skim milk
2 tablespoons grated Parmesan cheese
1½ teaspoons fresh oregano *or* ½ teaspoon dried oregano leaves
½ teaspoon paprika
¼ teaspoon ground black pepper

1 Place sesame seeds in small skillet. Cook over medium heat until light golden, stirring constantly. Set aside.

2 Cook pasta according to package directions, omitting salt. Drain and set aside.

3 Melt margarine in medium skillet. Add spinach and garlic; cook over medium heat until spinach is wilted. Stir in milk, cheese, oregano, paprika, black pepper and pasta. Cook over low heat until heated through. Sprinkle with sesame seeds; serve immediately.   *Makes 5 (½-cup) servings*

❖

Cook's Tip

Mildly sweet, nutty-tasting sesame seeds are commonly found in supermarket spice aisles. Because of their high oil content, sesame seeds can go rancid if kept for long at room temperature. For best results store them in the refrigerator or freezer.

❖

SOUTHERN GREENS AND PASTA

If you are unfamiliar with chicory's bitter-tasting leaves, then you may want to try the more subtle, yet still pungent mustard greens.

❖

Nutrients per Serving:

Calories	88
(13% of calories from fat)	
Total Fat	1 g
Saturated Fat	<1 g
Cholesterol	0 mg
Sodium	39 mg
Carbohydrate	15 g
Dietary Fiber	3 g
Protein	4 g
Calcium	31 mg
Iron	1 mg
Vitamin A	80 RE
Vitamin C	24 mg

DIETARY EXCHANGES:
1 Starch/Bread,
½ Vegetable

2 teaspoons olive oil
1 cup chopped green bell pepper
½ cup chopped onion
½ cup peeled and chopped jicama
⅓ cup chopped celery
1 clove garlic, minced
1 can (14 ounces) ⅓-less-salt chicken broth
2 tablespoons tomato paste
1 teaspoon dried oregano leaves
¼ teaspoon ground black pepper
1 package (10 ounces) frozen black-eyed peas
4 ounces uncooked radiatore or other medium pasta
1 head chicory, mustard greens or kale, washed, ribs removed, thinly sliced
2 to 3 drops red pepper sauce

1 Heat oil in large saucepan over medium heat. Add bell pepper, onion, jicama, celery and garlic. Cook and stir 3 minutes. Stir in chicken broth, tomato paste, oregano and black pepper. Bring to a boil; stir in black-eyed peas. Cover and simmer over low heat 20 minutes or until peas are tender.

2 Cook pasta according to package directions, omitting salt. Drain and set aside.

3 Add chicory to saucepan; cover and cook over low heat until wilted, about 3 minutes. Stir in pasta. Cook until heated through. Season to taste with red pepper sauce. Garnish as desired. *Makes 12 (½-cup) servings*

TEX-MEX NOODLE CAKE

❖

Noodle cakes are typically Oriental, but try this Tex-Mex version using angel hair pasta and you will insist it comes from the southwest!

❖

Nutrients per Serving:

Calories	183
(20% of calories from fat)	
Total Fat	4 g
Saturated Fat	<1 g
Cholesterol	36 mg
Sodium	136 mg
Carbohydrate	27 g
Dietary Fiber	2 g
Protein	9 g
Calcium	23 mg
Iron	2 mg
Vitamin A	67 RE
Vitamin C	18 mg

DIETARY EXCHANGES:
2 Starch/Bread, ½ Lean
Meat, ½ Fat

4 points

8 ounces uncooked angel hair pasta
½ cup finely chopped red bell pepper
1 whole egg plus 1 egg white
3 tablespoons grated Asiago or Parmesan cheese
2 tablespoons skim milk
2 teaspoons chili powder
½ teaspoon cumin
¼ teaspoon ground black pepper
  Plain nonfat yogurt
  Minced fresh cilantro

1 Cook pasta according to package directions, omitting salt. Drain and cool slightly, but do not rinse. Place pasta in medium bowl with bell pepper.

2 Combine whole egg, egg white, cheese, milk, chili powder, cumin and black pepper in small bowl; pour over pasta, tossing to coat evenly.

3 Spray large nonstick skillet with nonstick cooking spray. Add pasta mixture, spreading evenly and pressing firmly. Cook over medium-low heat until bottom is golden brown, about 7 to 8 minutes.

4 Slide noodle cake onto large plate, invert and return noodle cake to skillet. Cook until brown, 3 to 5 minutes.

5 Cut into wedges; serve warm, topped with yogurt and cilantro.

Makes 6 servings

PESTO-PASTA STUFFED TOMATOES

❖

This makes a wonderfully light accompaniment to any chicken or fish entrée.

❖

Nutrients per Serving:	
Calories	155
(33% of calories from fat)	
Total Fat	6 g
Saturated Fat	1 g
Cholesterol	2 mg
Sodium	154 mg
Carbohydrate	22 g
Dietary Fiber	3 g
Protein	6 g
Calcium	66 mg
Iron	1 mg
Vitamin A	195 RE
Vitamin C	27 mg

DIETARY EXCHANGES:
1 Starch/Bread, 1 Fat,
1½ Vegetable

3 points

3 ounces uncooked star or other small pasta
4 large tomatoes
1 cup loosely packed fresh basil
1 clove garlic, minced
3 tablespoons reduced calorie mayonnaise
1 tablespoon skim milk
¼ teaspoon ground black pepper
1 cup shredded zucchini
4 teaspoons grated Parmesan cheese

1 Cook pasta according to package directions, omitting salt. Drain and rinse; set aside.

2 Cut tops from tomatoes. Scoop out and discard all but ½ cup tomato pulp. Chop tomato pulp and add to pasta. Place tomatoes, cut side down, on paper towels; let drain 5 minutes.

3 Preheat oven to 350°F.

4 Place basil and garlic in blender or food processor; process until finely chopped. Add mayonnaise, milk and black pepper. Process until smooth.

5 Combine pasta mixture, zucchini and basil mixture; toss to coat evenly. Place tomatoes, cut side up, in 8-inch baking dish. Divide pasta mixture evenly among tomatoes, mounding filling slightly. Sprinkle with cheese.

6 Bake 10 to 15 minutes or until heated through.   *Makes 4 servings*

Marinated Artichokes & Shrimp in Citrus Vinaigrette (page 164)

APPETIZERS

CROSTINI

❖

These tasty little Tuscan treats are colorful and easy to make. Crostini are wonderful for last minute parties or unexpected guests because they can be made in minutes.

❖

¼ loaf whole wheat baguette (4 ounces)
4 plum tomatoes
1 cup (4 ounces) shredded part-skim mozzarella cheese
3 tablespoons prepared pesto sauce

1 Preheat oven to 400°F. Slice baguette into 16 very thin, diagonal slices. Slice each tomato vertically into four ¼-inch slices.

2 Place baguette slices on nonstick baking sheet. Top each with 1 tablespoon cheese, then 1 slice tomato. Bake about 8 minutes or until bread is lightly toasted and cheese is melted. Remove from oven; top each crostini with about ½ teaspoon pesto sauce. Garnish with fresh basil, if desired. Serve warm.   *Makes 8 appetizer servings*

Nutrients per Serving:

2 crostini

Calories	83
(34% of calories from fat)	
Total Fat	3 g
Saturated Fat	2 g
Cholesterol	9 mg
Sodium	159 mg
Carbohydrate	9 g
Dietary Fiber	<1 g
Protein	5 g
Calcium	121 mg
Iron	1 mg
Vitamin A	51 RE
Vitamin C	7 mg

DIETARY EXCHANGES:
½ Starch/Bread, ½ Lean Meat, ½ Fat

❖

Cook's Tip

Plum tomatoes, also called Roma tomatoes, are flavorful egg-shaped tomatoes that come in red and yellow varieties. As with other tomatoes, they are very perishable. Choose firm tomatoes that are fragrant and free of blemishes. Ripe tomatoes should be stored at room temperature and used within a few days.

❖

MARINATED ARTICHOKES & SHRIMP IN CITRUS VINAIGRETTE

Poaching the shrimp in orange juice adds a subtle and complementary flavor to the marinated artichoke hearts. This unique appetizer has only 2 grams of fat per serving and is high in vitamin C.

❖

Nutrients per Serving:

Calories	135
(14% of calories from fat)	
Total Fat	2 g
Saturated Fat	<1 g
Cholesterol	87 mg
Sodium	236 mg
Carbohydrate	19 g
Dietary Fiber	4 g
Protein	12 g
Calcium	69 mg
Iron	2 mg
Vitamin A	66 RE
Vitamin C	61 mg

DIETARY EXCHANGES:
1 Lean Meat, 1 Fruit,
1 Vegetable

VINAIGRETTE

  1 large seedless orange, peeled and sectioned
  3 tablespoons red wine vinegar
  3 tablespoons fat free mayonnaise
  1 teaspoon fresh thyme *or* ¼ teaspoon dried thyme leaves
  2 teaspoons extra virgin olive oil

SALAD

  1 package (9 ounces) frozen artichoke hearts, thawed
12 raw shrimp (12 ounces)
  1 cup orange juice

1 To prepare vinaigrette, place all vinaigrette ingredients except oil in blender or food processor; process until smooth. Pour mixture into medium nonmetal bowl and whisk in oil until well blended. Fold artichoke hearts into vinaigrette. Cover and refrigerate several hours or overnight.

2 Peel shrimp, leaving tails attached. Devein and butterfly shrimp. Bring orange juice to a boil in medium saucepan. Add shrimp and cook about 2 minutes or *just* until they turn pink and opaque.

3 To serve, place about 3 artichoke hearts on each of 6 plates. Top each serving with 2 shrimp. Drizzle vinaigrette over tops. Garnish with fresh Italian parsley, if desired.

Makes 6 appetizer servings

ROASTED EGGPLANT SPREAD WITH FOCACCIA

This no cholesterol appetizer is perfect for any Italian meal!

❖

Nutrients per Serving:

3 tablespoons eggplant spread with 3 wedges focaccia

Calories	127
(21% of calories from fat)	
Total Fat	3 g
Saturated Fat	<1 g
Cholesterol	0 mg
Sodium	267 mg
Carbohydrate	22 g
Dietary Fiber	3 g
Protein	4 g
Calcium	15 mg
Iron	1 mg
Vitamin A	12 RE
Vitamin C	4 mg

DIETARY EXCHANGES:
1½ Starch/Bread, ½ Fat

1 eggplant (1 pound)
1 medium tomato
1 tablespoon fresh lemon juice
1 tablespoon chopped fresh basil *or* 1 teaspoon dried basil leaves
2 teaspoons chopped fresh thyme *or* ¾ teaspoon dried thyme leaves
1 clove garlic, minced
¼ teaspoon salt
1 tablespoon extra virgin olive oil
   Focaccia (page 188)

1 Preheat oven to 400°F. Poke holes in several places in eggplant with fork. Cut stem end from tomato and place in small baking pan. Place eggplant on oven rack; bake 10 minutes. Place tomato in oven with eggplant. Bake vegetables 40 minutes.

2 Cool vegetables slightly, then peel. Cut eggplant into large slices. Place tomato and eggplant in food processor or blender. Add lemon juice, basil, thyme, garlic and salt; process until well blended. Slowly drizzle oil through feed tube and process until mixture is well blended. Refrigerate 3 hours or overnight.

3 To serve, spread 1 tablespoon on each focaccia wedge. Garnish with cherry tomato wedges and additional fresh basil, if desired.   *Makes 10 appetizer servings*

❖

Cook's Tip

When buying eggplants, look for firm eggplants with smooth skin and a uniform color. Avoid those that are soft, shriveled or have cuts or scars. Eggplants bruise easily. Handle gently and store at room temperature up to two days. Use as soon as possible since eggplants become bitter with age.

❖

PETITE PIZZAS

❖

This recipe includes two different toppings so that you can serve only pizza at your party and still offer a variety of appetizers.

❖

½ cup warm water (110° to 115°F)
¾ teaspoon active dry yeast
½ teaspoon sugar
¾ cup bread flour*
¾ cup whole wheat flour
¼ teaspoon salt
1½ teaspoons extra virgin olive oil
　 Pizza Sauce (page 170)
¼ cup finely chopped green bell pepper
¼ cup finely chopped onion
　2 ounces Italian turkey sausage, crumbled and cooked
⅔ cup sliced mushrooms, cooked until soft
¼ cup freshly grated Parmesan cheese
¼ cup (1 ounce) shredded part-skim mozzarella cheese

Nutrients per Serving:

*2 sausage pizzas and
2 mushroom pizzas*

Calories	148
(25% of calories from fat)	
Total Fat	4 g
Saturated Fat	1 g
Cholesterol	9 mg
Sodium	357 mg
Carbohydrate	22 g
Dietary Fiber	2 g
Protein	7 g
Calcium	88 mg
Iron	2 mg
Vitamin A	47 RE
Vitamin C	9 mg

DIETARY EXCHANGES:
1 Starch/Bread, ½ Lean
Meat, ½ Vegetable, ½ Fat

 To prepare crust, place warm water in small bowl. Sprinkle yeast and sugar on top; stir to combine. Let stand 10 minutes or until bubbly. Combine flours and salt in medium bowl. Stir in oil and yeast mixture; mix until smooth. Knead dough on lightly floured work surface 5 minutes or until smooth and elastic. Place dough in medium bowl sprayed with nonstick cooking spray. Turn dough so top is coated with cooking spray; cover with towel. Let rise in warm place 45 minutes or until doubled in bulk. Punch down dough; place on lightly floured surface and knead 2 minutes more. Cover with towel and let rise 20 minutes more. Roll out to ¼-inch thickness and cut into 32 circles with 2-inch cookie or biscuit cutter. Place on baking sheet sprayed with cooking spray. (Combine scraps and roll out again to obtain 32 circles, if necessary.)

2 Prepare Pizza Sauce. Place about ½ teaspoon sauce on each dough round. Spread sauce gently, leaving a small border of crust.

3 Preheat oven to 400°F. Combine bell pepper and onion in small bowl. Evenly sprinkle on top of sauce. Place sausage on half the pizzas and 1 or 2 mushroom slices on each of remaining pizzas. Evenly sprinkle cheeses on pizzas. Bake 10 minutes or until cheese melts. Serve immediately. (To reheat, warm pizzas in 250°F oven 10 minutes.) Garnish with fresh basil, if desired.   *Makes 8 appetizer servings*

*All-purpose flour may be substituted; however, bread flour works better with yeast since it contains more gluten. It also contains more vitamin C and potassium.

(continued on page 170)

Petite Pizzas, continued

PIZZA SAUCE

½ teaspoon extra virgin olive oil
1 clove garlic, minced
1 can (8 ounces) tomato sauce
1 tablespoon chopped fresh basil *or* 1 teaspoon dried basil leaves
½ teaspoon dried oregano leaves
    Dash salt and black pepper

1 Heat oil in small saucepan over medium heat. Add garlic; cook and stir 1 minute, being careful not to brown garlic. Add tomato sauce, basil and oregano; simmer 20 minutes. Stir in salt and black pepper.

CITRUS COOLER

2 cups fresh squeezed orange juice
2 cups unsweetened pineapple juice
1 teaspoon fresh lemon juice
¾ teaspoon vanilla extract
¾ teaspoon coconut extract
2 cups cold sparkling water

1 Combine juices and extracts in large pitcher; refrigerate until cold. Just before serving, stir in sparkling water and pour over ice. Garnish with lemon slices, if desired.

Makes 8 servings

This tropical nonalcoholic drink is refreshing and thirst quenching. It is also very high in vitamin C. This cooler is a wonderful alternative beverage for cocktail parties, and kids love it for their parties too.

Nutrients per Serving:

¾ cup

Calories	66
(2% of calories from fat)	
Total Fat	<1 g
Saturated Fat	<1 g
Cholesterol	0 mg
Sodium	2 mg
Carbohydrate	15 g
Dietary Fiber	1 g
Protein	1 g
Calcium	25 mg
Iron	<1 mg
Vitamin A	13 RE
Vitamin C	38 mg

DIETARY EXCHANGES:
1 Fruit

GINGERED CHICKEN POT STICKERS

These Asian tidbits are also great on steamed rice as an entrée. For a meatless dish, substitute tempeh, found in Asian markets, for the chicken.

Nutrients per Serving:

3 pot stickers

Calories	111
(20% of calories from fat)	
Total Fat	2 g
Saturated Fat	<1 g
Cholesterol	11 mg
Sodium	303 mg
Carbohydrate	16 g
Dietary Fiber	<1 g
Protein	6 g
Calcium	27 mg
Iron	1 mg
Vitamin A	20 RE
Vitamin C	12 mg

DIETARY EXCHANGES:
1 Starch/Bread, ½ Lean Meat

  3 cups finely shredded cabbage
  1 egg white, lightly beaten
  1 tablespoon citrus-seasoned soy sauce or light soy sauce
  ¼ teaspoon crushed red pepper
  1 tablespoon minced fresh ginger
  4 green onions with tops, finely chopped
  ¼ pound ground chicken breast, cooked and drained
 24 wonton wrappers, at room temperature
    Cornstarch
  ½ cup water
  1 tablespoon oyster sauce
  ½ teaspoon honey
  ⅛ teaspoon crushed red pepper
  2 teaspoons grated lemon peel
  1 tablespoon peanut oil

1 Steam cabbage 5 minutes, then cool to room temperature. Squeeze out any excess moisture; set aside.

2 To prepare filling, combine egg white, soy sauce, ¼ teaspoon red pepper, ginger and green onions in large bowl; blend well. Stir in cabbage and chicken.

3 To prepare pot stickers, place 1 tablespoon filling in center of 1 wonton wrapper. Gather edges around filling, pressing firmly at top to seal. Repeat with remaining wrappers and filling. Place pot stickers on large baking sheet dusted with cornstarch. Refrigerate 1 hour or until cold.

4 Meanwhile, to prepare sauce, combine remaining ingredients except oil in small bowl; mix well. Set aside.

5 Heat oil in large nonstick skillet over high heat. Add pot stickers and cook until bottoms are golden brown. Pour sauce over top. Cover and cook 3 minutes. Uncover and cook until all liquid is absorbed. Serve warm on tray as finger food or on small plates with chopsticks as first course.　　　*Makes 8 appetizer servings*

COLD ASPARAGUS WITH LEMON-MUSTARD DRESSING

❖

This easy-to-make, no cholesterol first course may be served either as an appetizer at the table or with cocktails as an hors d'oeuvre. If you plan to serve it as an hors d'oeuvre, the asparagus spears may be served with the sauce separately for dipping.

◆

12 fresh asparagus spears
 2 tablespoons fat free mayonnaise
 1 tablespoon sweet brown mustard
 1 tablespoon fresh lemon juice
 1 teaspoon grated lemon peel, divided

1 Steam asparagus until crisp-tender and bright green; immediately drain and run under cold water. Cover and refrigerate until chilled.

2 Combine mayonnaise, mustard and lemon juice in small bowl; blend well. Stir in ½ teaspoon lemon peel; set aside.

3 Divide asparagus between 2 plates. Spoon 2 tablespoons dressing over top of each serving; sprinkle each with ¼ teaspoon lemon peel. Garnish with carrot strips and edible flowers, such as pansies, violets or nasturtiums, if desired.

Makes 2 appetizer servings

Nutrients per Serving:

Calories	39
(14% of calories from fat)	
Total Fat	1 g
Saturated Fat	<1 g
Cholesterol	0 mg
Sodium	294 mg
Carbohydrate	7 g
Dietary Fiber	2 g
Protein	3 g
Calcium	33 mg
Iron	1 mg
Vitamin A	71 RE
Vitamin C	15 mg

DIETARY EXCHANGES:
1½ Vegetable

❖

Health Note

Asparagus is a great source of glutathione, a powerful antioxidant.
Studies have shown that glutathione acts against at least
30 carcinogens.

❖

TINY SEAFOOD TOSTADAS WITH BLACK BEAN DIP

Nonstick cooking spray
4 (8-inch) whole wheat or flour tortillas, cut into 32 (2½-inch) rounds or other shapes
1 cup Black Bean Dip (recipe follows)
1 cup shredded fresh spinach
¾ cup tiny cooked or canned shrimp
¾ cup salsa
½ cup (2 ounces) shredded reduced fat Monterey Jack cheese
¼ cup light sour cream

1 Preheat oven to 350°F. Spray cooking spray on baking sheet. Place tortilla rounds evenly on prepared baking sheet. Lightly spray tortillas with cooking spray and bake 10 minutes. Turn over and spray again; bake 3 minutes more. Prepare Black Bean Dip.

2 To prepare tostadas, spread each toasted tortilla with 1½ teaspoons Black Bean Dip. Layer each with 1½ teaspoons shredded spinach, 1 teaspoon shrimp, 1 teaspoon salsa, a sprinkle of cheese and a dab of sour cream. Garnish with thin green chili strips or fresh cilantro, if desired. Serve immediately. *Makes 8 appetizer servings*

Nutrients per Serving:	
4 tostadas	
Calories	157
(20% of calories from fat)	
Total Fat	4 g
Saturated Fat	1 g
Cholesterol	31 mg
Sodium	747 mg
Carbohydrate	23 g
Dietary Fiber	4 g
Protein	12 g
Calcium	117 mg
Iron	1 mg
Vitamin A	148 RE
Vitamin C	21 mg

DIETARY EXCHANGES:
1 Starch/Bread, 1 Lean Meat, 1 Vegetable

❖

BLACK BEAN DIP

1 can (15 ounces) black beans, undrained
1 teaspoon chili powder
¼ teaspoon *each* salt, black pepper and ground cumin
2 drops hot pepper sauce
¾ cup minced white onion
2 cloves garlic, minced
1 can (4 ounces) chopped green chilies, drained
   Corn Tortilla Chips (page 182) and raw jicama sticks (optional)

1 Drain beans, reserving 2 tablespoons liquid. Combine beans, reserved liquid, chili powder, salt, black pepper, cumin and hot pepper sauce in blender; process until smooth. Combine onion and garlic in nonstick skillet; cover and cook over low heat until onion is soft. Uncover and cook until slightly browned. Add chilies; cook 3 minutes more. Add bean mixture; mix well. Serve hot or cold with chips and jicama; garnish with pepper strips, if desired. *Makes about 24 appetizer servings*

Nutrients per Serving:	
1 tablespoon	
Calories	18
(7% of calories from fat)	
Total Fat	<1 g
Saturated Fat	<1 g
Cholesterol	0 mg
Sodium	134 mg
Carbohydrate	4 g
Dietary Fiber	1 g
Protein	2 g
Calcium	3 mg
Iron	<1 mg
Vitamin A	7 RE
Vitamin C	4 mg

DIETARY EXCHANGES:
½ Starch/Bread

MINTED MELON SOUP

❖

When possible, make the mint syrup the day before you plan to make the soup. After cooling the syrup to room temperature, store it in an airtight container in the refrigerator with the mint and basil. Strain the liquid just before adding to the soup. This intensifies the subtle flavor and makes this delicious and refreshing soup even better.

❖

1 cup water
1 tablespoon sugar
1½ cups fresh mint, including stems
2 fresh basil leaves
1½ cups diced cantaloupe
4 teaspoons fresh lemon juice, divided
1½ cups diced and seeded watermelon

1 Combine water and sugar in small saucepan; mix well. Bring to a boil over medium heat. Add mint and basil; simmer 10 minutes or until reduced by two-thirds. Remove from heat; cover and let stand at least 2 hours or until cool. Strain liquid; set aside.

2 Place cantaloupe in blender or food processor; process until smooth. Add 2 tablespoons mint syrup and 2 teaspoons lemon juice. Blend to mix well. Pour into airtight container. Cover and refrigerate until cold. Repeat procedure with watermelon, 2 teaspoons mint syrup and remaining 2 teaspoons lemon juice. Discard any remaining mint syrup.

3 To serve, simultaneously pour ¼ cup of each melon soup, side by side, into a serving bowl. Place 1 mint sprig in center for garnish, if desired. Repeat with remaining soup.

Makes 4 appetizer servings

Nutrients per Serving:	
Calories	48
(7% of calories from fat)	
Total Fat	<1 g
Saturated Fat	0 g
Cholesterol	0 mg
Sodium	7 mg
Carbohydrate	11 g
Dietary Fiber	1 g
Protein	1 g
Calcium	12 mg
Iron	<1 mg
Vitamin A	216 RE
Vitamin C	33 mg

DIETARY EXCHANGES:
1 Fruit

❖

Entertaining Tip

Select the entrée first, then plan the other dishes around it. Pick foods with a variety of color, texture and contrasting flavors for good eye and taste appeal. A monochromatic meal is not only visually uninteresting, but is usually perceived as less flavorful.

❖

POLENTA TRIANGLES

❖

This recipe uses corn grits rather than cornmeal because corn grits give the polenta a heartier texture. Yellow grits have a nice golden color; however, white corn grits are more readily available and may be substituted. You can find grits in most supermarket cereal aisles.

❖

½ cup yellow corn grits
1½ cups chicken broth, divided
 2 cloves garlic, minced
½ cup (2 ounces) crumbled feta cheese
 1 red bell pepper, roasted,* peeled and finely chopped
   Nonstick cooking spray

1 Combine grits and ½ cup broth; mix well and set aside. Pour remaining 1 cup broth into heavy large saucepan; bring to a boil. Add garlic and moistened grits; mix well and return to a boil. Reduce heat to low; cover and cook 20 minutes. Remove from heat; add feta cheese. Stir until cheese is completely melted. Add red pepper; mix well.

2 Spray 8-inch square pan with cooking spray. Spoon grits mixture into prepared pan. Press grits evenly into pan with wet fingertips. Refrigerate until cold.

3 Preheat broiler. Turn polenta out onto cutting board and cut into 2-inch squares. Cut each square diagonally into 2 triangles. Spray baking sheet with cooking spray. Place polenta triangles on prepared baking sheet and spray tops lightly with cooking spray. Place under broiler until lightly browned. Turn triangles over and broil until browned and crisp. Serve warm or at room temperature. Garnish with fresh oregano and chives, if desired.

Makes 8 appetizer servings

*Place pepper on foil-lined broiler pan; broil 15 minutes or until blackened on all sides, turning every 5 minutes. Place pepper in paper bag; close bag and let stand 15 minutes before peeling.

Nutrients per Serving:

6 triangles

Calories	62
(26% of calories from fat)	
Total Fat	2 g
Saturated Fat	1 g
Cholesterol	6 mg
Sodium	142 mg
Carbohydrate	9 g
Dietary Fiber	<1 g
Protein	3 g
Calcium	37 mg
Iron	1 mg
Vitamin A	26 RE
Vitamin C	7 mg

DIETARY EXCHANGES:
1 Starch/Bread

SPICED APPLE TEA

Nutrients per Serving:

about 1 cup

Calories	55
(0% of calories from fat)	
Total Fat	0 g
Saturated Fat	0 g
Cholesterol	0 mg
Sodium	5 mg
Carbohydrate	14 g
Dietary Fiber	<1 g
Protein	0 g
Calcium	4 mg
Iron	1 mg
Vitamin A	0 RE
Vitamin C	0 mg

DIETARY EXCHANGES:
1 Fruit

❖

2 cups unsweetened apple juice
6 whole cloves
1 cinnamon stick
3 cups water
3 bags cinnamon herbal tea

1 Combine juice, cloves and cinnamon stick in small saucepan. Bring to a boil over high heat. Reduce heat to low; simmer 10 minutes.

2 Meanwhile, place water in medium saucepan. Bring to a boil over high heat. Remove from heat; drop in tea bags and allow to steep for 6 minutes. Remove and discard tea bags.

3 Strain juice mixture; discard spices. Stir juice mixture into tea. Serve warm with additional cinnamon sticks, if desired *or* refrigerate and serve cold over ice. (Tea may be made ahead and reheated.)

Makes 4 servings

CORN TORTILLA CHIPS

Nutrients per Serving:

6 chips

Calories	57
(10% of calories from fat)	
Total Fat	1 g
Saturated Fat	<1 g
Cholesterol	0 mg
Sodium	40 mg
Carbohydrate	12 g
Dietary Fiber	0 g
Protein	1 g
Calcium	47 mg
Iron	<1 mg
Vitamin A	1 RE
Vitamin C	<1 mg

DIETARY EXCHANGES:
1 Starch/Bread

6 corn tortillas
   Nonstick cooking spray
½ teaspoon dried oregano leaves
¼ teaspoon ground cumin

1 Preheat oven to 400°F. Cut each tortilla into 6 triangles with pizza cutter or sharp knife. Place on baking sheet in a single layer.

2 Spray tortilla triangles lightly with cooking spray and quickly sprinkle evenly with oregano and cumin.

3 Immediately bake 5 to 10 minutes until edges are golden brown and chips are crispy. (Do not make these the day before serving; they will become soft if they sit too long.)

Makes 6 appetizer servings

Note: Recipe pictured on pages 177 and 209.

BREADS

MINIATURE FRUIT MUFFINS

These high fiber, nearly fat free muffins are just as delicious as they are appealing in appearance. Dividing the basic batter into thirds allows you to offer your guests three choices.

1 cup whole wheat flour
¾ cup all-purpose flour
½ cup firmly packed dark brown sugar
2 teaspoons baking powder
½ teaspoon baking soda
¼ teaspoon salt
1 cup buttermilk, divided
¾ cup frozen blueberries
1 small ripe banana, mashed
¼ teaspoon vanilla extract
⅓ cup unsweetened applesauce
2 tablespoons raisins
½ teaspoon ground cinnamon

1 Preheat oven to 400°F. Spray 36 miniature muffin cups with nonstick cooking spray.

2 Combine flours, brown sugar, baking powder, baking soda and salt in medium bowl. Place ⅔ cup dry ingredients in each of 2 small bowls.

3 To one portion of flour mixture, add ⅓ cup buttermilk and blueberries. Stir just until blended; spoon into 12 prepared muffin cups. To second portion, add ⅓ cup buttermilk, banana and vanilla. Stir just until blended; spoon into 12 muffin cups. To final portion, add remaining ⅓ cup buttermilk, applesauce, raisins and cinnamon. Stir just until blended; spoon into 12 muffin cups.

4 Bake 18 minutes or until lightly browned and wooden pick inserted into centers comes out clean. Cool slightly before serving. *Makes 12 servings*

Nutrients per Serving:

*3 miniature muffins
(1 blueberry, 1 banana,
1 applesauce raisin)*

Calories	130
(4% of calories from fat)	
Total Fat	1 g
Saturated Fat	<1 g
Cholesterol	1 mg
Sodium	178 mg
Carbohydrate	29 g
Dietary Fiber	2 g
Protein	3 g
Calcium	49 mg
Iron	1 mg
Vitamin A	4 RE
Vitamin C	2 mg

DIETARY EXCHANGES:
1 Starch/Bread, 1 Fruit

WHOLE WHEAT HERB BREAD

Nutrients per Serving:

Calories	99
(18% of calories from fat)	
Total Fat	2 g
Saturated Fat	<1 g
Cholesterol	<1 mg
Sodium	101 mg
Carbohydrate	17 g
Dietary Fiber	3 g
Protein	4 g
Calcium	18 mg
Iron	1 mg
Vitamin A	5 RE
Vitamin C	<1 mg

DIETARY EXCHANGES:
1 Starch/Bread, ½ Fat

❖

⅔ cup water
⅔ cup skim milk
2 teaspoons sugar
2 envelopes active dry yeast
3 egg whites, lightly beaten
3 tablespoons olive oil
1 teaspoon salt
½ teaspoon *each* dried basil leaves and dried oregano leaves
4 to 4½ cups whole wheat flour

1 Bring water to a boil in small saucepan. Remove from heat; stir in milk and sugar. When mixture is warm (110° to 115°F), add yeast. (Water at higher temperatures will kill the yeast.) Mix well; let stand 10 minutes or until bubbly.

2 Combine egg whites, oil, salt, basil and oregano in large bowl until well blended. Add yeast mixture; mix well. Add 4 cups flour, ½ cup at a time, mixing well after each addition, until dough is no longer sticky. Knead about 5 minutes or until smooth and elastic, adding more flour if dough is sticky. Form into a ball. Cover and let rise in warm place about 1 hour or until doubled in bulk.

3 Preheat oven to 350°F. Punch dough down and place on lightly floured surface. Divide into 4 pieces and roll each piece into a ball. Lightly spray baking sheet with nonstick cooking spray. Place dough balls on prepared baking sheet. Bake 30 to 35 minutes until golden brown and loaves sound hollow when tapped with finger.

Makes 24 servings

Nutrients per Serving:

1 tablespoon

Calories	28
(1% of calories from fat)	
Total Fat	<1 g
Saturated Fat	<1 g
Cholesterol	0 mg
Sodium	1 mg
Carbohydrate	7 g
Dietary Fiber	1 g
Protein	<1 g
Calcium	4 mg
Iron	<1 mg
Vitamin A	64 RE
Vitamin C	<1 mg

DIETARY EXCHANGES:
½ Fruit

APRICOT BUTTER

1 cup dried apricots (5 ounces)
1 cup unsweetened apple juice

1 Combine apricots and juice in small saucepan; bring to a boil over medium-high heat. Reduce heat to low; cover and simmer 20 minutes, stirring occasionally. Remove from heat; cool slightly. Pour mixture into blender or food processor; process until smooth. Cool to room temperature and refrigerate in airtight container or jar with tight fitting lid up to 3 months.

Makes 16 servings

FOCACCIA

❖

This focaccia is made into three small rounds rather than one large round so it may be cut into small pie-shaped wedges for spreading or dipping as an appetizer. This recipe calls for whole wheat flour to increase the fiber content. Recipe pictured on page 167.

❖

Nutrients per Serving:

3 wedges

Calories	102
(15% of calories from fat)	
Total Fat	2 g
Saturated Fat	<1 g
Cholesterol	0 mg
Sodium	214 mg
Carbohydrate	19 g
Dietary Fiber	2 g
Protein	3 g
Calcium	9 mg
Iron	1 mg
Vitamin A	<1 RE
Vitamin C	<1 mg

DIETARY EXCHANGES:
1½ Starch/Bread

¾ cup warm water (110° to 115°F)*
1½ teaspoons sugar
1 teaspoon active dry yeast
1 tablespoon extra virgin olive oil
1 teaspoon salt
1 teaspoon dried rosemary
1 cup all-purpose flour
1 cup whole wheat flour
Nonstick cooking spray

1 Pour water into large bowl. Dissolve sugar and yeast in water; let stand 10 minutes or until bubbly. Stir in oil, salt and rosemary. Add flours, ½ cup at a time, stirring until dough begins to pull away from side of bowl and forms a ball.

2 Turn dough onto lightly floured surface and knead 5 minutes or until dough is smooth and elastic, adding more flour if necessary. Place dough in bowl lightly sprayed with cooking spray and turn dough so all sides are coated. Cover with towel or plastic wrap and let rise in warm draft-free place about 1 hour or until doubled in bulk.

3 Turn dough onto lightly floured surface and knead 1 minute. Divide into 3 balls; roll each into 6-inch circle. Using fingertips, dimple surfaces of dough. Place on baking sheet sprayed with cooking spray; cover and let rise 30 minutes more.

4 Preheat oven to 400°F. Spray tops of dough circles with cooking spray; bake about 13 minutes or until golden brown. Remove from oven and cut each loaf into 10 wedges.

Makes 10 servings

*Water at higher temperatures will kill the yeast.

GARLIC BREAD

Both the taste and texture of good sourdough bread are perfect for this savory hot bread. Adding just a small amount of extra virgin olive oil to the roasted garlic prevents the bread from getting dry. Recipe pictured on page 201.

6 whole heads of garlic
1 teaspoon dried oregano leaves
4½ teaspoons extra virgin olive oil
1 loaf, unsliced, crusty sourdough or French bread, cut horizontally in half (1½ pounds)
Black pepper

 1 Preheat oven to 350°F. Cut tops off heads of garlic and peel each head. Place heads, cut sides up, in small baking pan and sprinkle with oregano. Cover tightly with foil and bake 30 minutes. Uncover and bake 30 minutes more. Remove from oven; cool until easy to handle.

2 Carefully squeeze soft roasted garlic out of each clove to yield about ¾ cup. Place in blender or food processor; add oil and process until smooth.

3 Spread garlic mixture evenly on both halves of bread and sprinkle lightly with black pepper. Place halves together and cut loaf vertically into 8 equal pieces, being careful to keep loaf intact. Wrap tightly in foil. Bake 30 minutes.

4 To serve, unwrap loaf leaving foil crushed around outside to keep warm.

Makes 16 servings

Nutrients per Serving:

1 piece

Calories	149
(16% of calories from fat)	
Total Fat	3 g
Saturated Fat	<1 g
Cholesterol	0 mg
Sodium	261 mg
Carbohydrate	27 g
Dietary Fiber	<1 g
Protein	5 g
Calcium	58 mg
Iron	1 mg
Vitamin A	1 RE
Vitamin C	4 mg

DIETARY EXCHANGES:
1½ Starch/Bread,
1 Vegetable, ½ Fat

Health Note
Garlic has been shown to lower blood-cholesterol levels and also contains multiple antioxidants and immune-system boosters. Garlic also acts as an effective decongestant and anti-inflammatory agent, making it a good cold medication. Some studies have even shown that garlic can kill bacteria, acting as an antibiotic.

ROSEMARY BREAD STICKS

These amusing looking and low fat bread sticks are real conversation pieces as well as being simply delicious. They are also so easy to make that you may find them a fun addition to many menus. Try other herb and spice variations, such as thyme or cumin, in place of the rosemary.

⅔ cup 2% low fat milk
¼ cup finely chopped fresh chives
2 teaspoons baking powder
1 teaspoon finely chopped fresh rosemary or dried rosemary
¾ teaspoon salt
½ teaspoon black pepper
¾ cup whole wheat flour
¾ cup all-purpose flour
   Nonstick cooking spray

1 Combine milk, chives, baking powder, rosemary, salt and black pepper in large bowl; mix well. Stir in flours, ½ cup at a time, until blended. Turn onto floured surface and knead dough about 5 minutes or until smooth and elastic, adding a little more flour if dough is sticky. Let stand 30 minutes at room temperature.

2 Preheat oven to 375°F. Spray baking sheet with cooking spray.

3 Divide dough into 12 equal balls, about 1¼ ounces each. Roll each ball into long thin rope and place on prepared baking sheet. Lightly spray bread sticks with cooking spray.

4 Bake about 12 minutes or until bottoms are golden brown. Turn bread sticks over and bake about 10 minutes more or until other side is browned.

Makes 12 bread sticks

Nutrients per Serving:

1 bread stick

Calories	62
(7% of calories from fat)	
Total Fat	1 g
Saturated Fat	<1 g
Cholesterol	1 mg
Sodium	196 mg
Carbohydrate	12 g
Dietary Fiber	1 g
Protein	2 g
Calcium	33 mg
Iron	1 mg
Vitamin A	13 RE
Vitamin C	1 mg

DIETARY EXCHANGES:
1 Starch/Bread

Entertaining Tip

Not every item on the menu needs to be a showstopper. Select one or two involved recipes and let the remainder be store-bought or easy to make ahead. Many guests like to bring a dessert or appetizer. Be sure to have some ideas ready so you may offer suggestions that complement the meal.

ENTREES

VEGETABLE RISOTTO

❖

This tasty Italian rice dish contains almost no cholesterol since it is made with olive oil instead of butter.

❖

2 cups broccoli flowerets
1 cup finely chopped zucchini
1 cup finely chopped yellow squash
1 cup finely chopped red bell pepper
2½ cups chicken broth
1 tablespoon extra virgin olive oil
2 tablespoons finely chopped onion
½ cup Arborio or other short-grain rice
¼ cup dry white wine or water
⅓ cup freshly grated Parmesan cheese

1 Steam broccoli, zucchini, yellow squash and bell pepper 3 minutes or just until crisp-tender. Rinse with cold water; drain and set aside.

2 Bring broth to a simmer in small saucepan; keep hot on low heat.

3 Heat oil in heavy large saucepan over medium-high heat until hot. Add onion; reduce heat to medium. Cook and stir about 5 minutes or until onion is translucent. Add rice, stirring to coat with oil. Add wine; cook and stir until almost dry. Add ½ cup hot broth; cook and stir until broth is absorbed. Continue adding broth, ½ cup at a time, allowing broth to absorb before each addition and stirring frequently. (Total cooking time for broth absorption is about 20 minutes.)

4 Remove from heat and stir in cheese. Add steamed vegetables and mix well. Serve immediately.

Makes 6 servings

Nutrients per Serving:

Calories	150
(27% of calories from fat)	
Total Fat	5 g
Saturated Fat	1 g
Cholesterol	4 mg
Sodium	253 mg
Carbohydrate	20 g
Dietary Fiber	2 g
Protein	7 g
Calcium	107 mg
Iron	2 mg
Vitamin A	93 RE
Vitamin C	59 mg

DIETARY EXCHANGES:
1 Starch/Bread,
1 Vegetable, 1 Fat

SALMON EN PAPILLOTE

❖

To eliminate last minute clean up before your guest arrives, prepare this dish in advance and refrigerate until you are ready to cook. The Dilled Wine Sauce may either be spooned into the package when you open it or served on the side.

❖

¾ cup water
 1 teaspoon extra virgin olive oil
¼ teaspoon salt
⅛ teaspoon black pepper
½ cup couscous
   Parchment paper
 1 small yellow squash, cut into julienned strips (1 cup)
½ pound fresh salmon fillet, bones removed and cut into 2 pieces
½ cup peeled and diced plum tomatoes
 2 teaspoons *each* chopped fresh dill and chopped fresh tarragon *or*
      ¼ teaspoon *each* dried dill weed and dried tarragon leaves
 2 teaspoons *each* chopped fresh chives and chopped fresh parsley
 1 egg, beaten
   Dilled Wine Sauce (page 196)

1 Preheat oven to 350°F. To prepare couscous, combine water, oil, salt and black pepper in small saucepan with tight fitting lid. Bring to a boil. Add couscous and mix well. Cover and remove from heat. Let stand 5 minutes or until all liquid is absorbed.

2 Make 2 large hearts with 2 sheets parchment paper by folding each piece in half and cutting into half-heart shape. Unfold hearts and spoon ½ cup couscous on one side of each heart. Top each with ½ cup squash, 1 piece salmon, ¼ cup tomato and 1 teaspoon *each* dill, tarragon, chives and parsley. To seal packages, brush outer edges of hearts with beaten egg. Fold over again making half-heart shapes; press edges together, crimping tightly with fingers. Place packages on ungreased baking sheet; bake 14 minutes. Meanwhile, prepare Dilled Wine Sauce.

3 To serve, place each package on large plate and cut an "X" in top. Fold corners back and drizzle sauce over each serving. Garnish with edible flowers, such as pansies, violets or nasturtiums, if desired.

Makes 2 servings

(continued on page 196)

Salmon en Papillote, continued

Nutrients per Serving:

includes ¼ cup sauce

Calories	497
(26% of calories from fat)	
Total Fat	14 g
Saturated Fat	3 g
Cholesterol	127 mg
Sodium	387 mg
Carbohydrate	54 g
Dietary Fiber	11 g
Protein	29 g
Calcium	131 mg
Iron	4 mg
Vitamin A	146 RE
Vitamin C	24 mg

DIETARY EXCHANGES:
3 Starch/Bread, 3 Lean
Meat, 2 Vegetable, 1½ Fat

DILLED WINE SAUCE

1½ cups finely chopped onions
1 tablespoon dried dill weed *or* ½ cup chopped fresh dill
1½ teaspoons dried tarragon leaves *or* ¼ cup chopped fresh tarragon
1 clove garlic, peeled and quartered
½ cup dry white wine
2 teaspoons extra virgin olive oil

1 Combine all ingredients except oil in blender or food processor; process until smooth.

2 Pour dill mixture into small saucepan and bring to a boil over medium heat. Reduce heat to low; simmer until reduced by half. Strain sauce into small bowl, pressing all liquid through strainer with back of spoon. Slowly whisk in oil until smooth and well blended.

Makes ½ cup

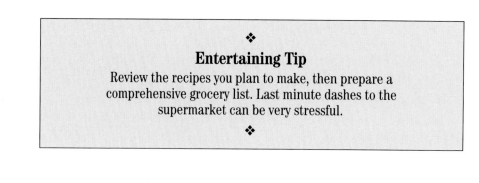

❖

Entertaining Tip

Review the recipes you plan to make, then prepare a comprehensive grocery list. Last minute dashes to the supermarket can be very stressful.

❖

RACK OF LAMB WITH DIJON-MUSTARD SAUCE

❖

If you prefer really rare lamb turn the oven off after just 5 minutes, or if you like your lamb well done leave the oven on for 10 to 12 minutes. You may leave the lamb in the oven for more than 30 minutes; what is crucial is that you turn off the oven at the correct time. This allows the host or hostess more time with the guests. Recipe pictured on page 191.

❖

1 rack of lamb (3 pounds), all visible fat removed
1 cup finely chopped fresh parsley
½ cup Dijon-style mustard
½ cup soft whole wheat bread crumbs
1 tablespoon chopped fresh rosemary *or* 2 teaspoons dried rosemary
1 teaspoon minced garlic
Rosemary Bread Sticks (page 190)

1 Preheat oven to 500°F. Place lamb in large baking pan.

2 Combine parsley, mustard, bread crumbs, rosemary and garlic in small bowl. Spread evenly over top of lamb. Place in center of oven; cook 7 minutes for medium-rare. *Turn off oven but do not open door for at least 30 minutes.*

3 Serve 2 to 3 chops on each plate, depending on size and total number of chops. Serve with Rosemary Bread Sticks. Garnish with additional fresh rosemary, lemon slices and lemon peel strips, if desired. *Makes 6 servings*

Nutrients per Serving:

4 ounces lamb with 2 bread sticks

Calories	437
(37% of calories from fat)	
Total Fat	18 g
Saturated Fat	6 g
Cholesterol	111 mg
Sodium	790 mg
Carbohydrate	28 g
Dietary Fiber	3 g
Protein	40 g
Calcium	131 mg
Iron	5 mg
Vitamin A	71 RE
Vitamin C	14 mg

DIETARY EXCHANGES:
2 Starch/Bread, 4 Lean Meat, 1½ Fat

❖

Entertaining Tip

Do not invite more people than you can comfortably seat at your table. Guests may become uncomfortable if the table is crowded. Also, make sure you have enough serving dishes and utensils.

❖

EGGS PRIMAVERA

❖

The bread bowls make an elegant and unusual presentation for these tasty eggs. This dish may also be served by itself accompanied by a basket of rolls and an assortment of fresh fruit for another wonderful brunch menu.

❖

4 round loaves (4 inches) Whole Wheat Herb Bread (page 186)*
  Nonstick cooking spray
1½ cups chopped onions
¾ cup chopped yellow squash
¾ cup chopped zucchini
½ cup chopped red bell pepper
2 ounces snow peas, trimmed and cut into thirds diagonally
¼ cup finely chopped fresh parsley
1½ teaspoons finely chopped fresh thyme *or* ¾ teaspoon dried thyme leaves
1 teaspoon finely chopped fresh rosemary *or* ½ teaspoon dried rosemary
2 whole eggs
4 egg whites
¼ teaspoon black pepper
½ cup (2 ounces) shredded reduced fat Swiss cheese

1 Preheat oven to 350°F. Slice top off each loaf of bread. Carefully hollow out each loaf, leaving walls ½ inch thick. Reserve centers for another use, such as croutons or bread crumbs. Place loaves and tops, cut sides up, on baking sheet. Spray all surfaces with cooking spray; bake 15 minutes or until well toasted.

2 Meanwhile, spray large nonstick skillet with cooking spray and heat over medium heat until hot. Add onions; cook and stir 3 minutes or until soft. Add yellow squash, zucchini and bell pepper; cook and stir 3 minutes or until crisp-tender. Add snow peas, parsley, thyme and rosemary; cook and stir 1 minute. Whisk whole eggs, egg whites and black pepper in small bowl until blended. Add to vegetable mixture; gently stir until eggs begin to set. Sprinkle cheese over top; gently stir until cheese melts and eggs are set but not dry.

3 Fill each bread bowl with ¼ of egg filling mixture, about 1 cup. Place tops back on bread bowls off center so filling shows. Place on serving plates.   *Makes 4 servings*

*Bread bowls are optional. Omit step 1, if desired, and divide eggs among 4 serving plates and serve with desired bread or rolls.

Nutrients per Serving:

¼ *egg mixture with 1 ounce of bread*

Calories	201
(26% of calories from fat)	
Total Fat	6 g
Saturated Fat	2 g
Cholesterol	114 mg
Sodium	336 mg
Carbohydrate	23 g
Dietary Fiber	4 g
Protein	14 g
Calcium	170 mg
Iron	2 mg
Vitamin A	116 RE
Vitamin C	46 mg

DIETARY EXCHANGES:
1 Starch/Bread, 1½ Lean Meat, 1 Vegetable, ½ Fat

GRILLED MARINATED CHICKEN

❖

Although dark meat has more fat than white meat, removing the skin before grilling eliminates a lot of the fat. By marinating the chicken overnight in this tasty fat free marinade, the chicken stays moist even without the skin.

❖

8 chicken hind quarters (thigh and drumsticks attached)
6 ounces frozen lemonade concentrate, thawed
2 tablespoons white wine vinegar
1 tablespoon grated lemon peel
2 cloves garlic, minced
  Garlic Bread (page 189)

1 Remove skin and all visible fat from chicken. Place chicken in 13×9-inch glass baking dish. Combine all remaining ingredients except Garlic Bread in small bowl, blending well. Pour over chicken. Cover and refrigerate 3 hours or overnight, turning chicken occasionally.

2 Lightly coat grid of grill with vegetable cooking spray. Heat grill until coals are glowing. Place chicken on grill and cook 10 to 15 minutes per side or until juices run clear when pierced with fork and chicken is no longer pink near bone. (Do not overcook or chicken will be dry.) Serve with Garlic Bread. Garnish with curly endive and lemon peel strips, if desired.
Makes 8 servings

Nutrients per Serving:

*1 chicken quarter with
2 pieces Garlic Bread*

Calories	518
(28% of calories from fat)	
Total Fat	16 g
Saturated Fat	4 g
Cholesterol	93 mg
Sodium	609 mg
Carbohydrate	57 g
Dietary Fiber	1 g
Protein	35 g
Calcium	129 mg
Iron	4 mg
Vitamin A	21 RE
Vitamin C	11 mg

DIETARY EXCHANGES:
4 Starch/Bread, 3½ Lean
Meat, ½ Vegetable, ½ Fat

❖

Cook's Tip

To easily peel garlic, place a clove on a cutting board. Cover the clove with the flat side of a chef's knife blade, then firmly press down on the blade with your fist. This loosens the skin so that it comes right off.

❖

CHEDDAR CHEESE STRATA

This make-ahead marvel is perfect for entertaining. You may make it the night before and have your entrée ready in just one hour the day of your party.

1 pound French bread, cut into ½- to ¾-inch slices, crusts removed, divided
2 cups (8 ounces) shredded reduced fat Cheddar cheese, divided
2 whole eggs
3 egg whites
1 quart skim milk
1 teaspoon grated fresh onion
1 teaspoon dry mustard
½ teaspoon salt
　Paprika to taste

1 Spray 13×9-inch glass baking dish with nonstick cooking spray. Place half the bread slices in bottom of prepared dish, overlapping slightly if necessary. Sprinkle with 1¼ cups cheese. Place remaining bread slices on top of cheese.

2 Whisk whole eggs and egg whites in large bowl. Add milk, onion, mustard and salt; whisk until well blended. Pour evenly over bread and cheese. Cover with remaining ¾ cup cheese and sprinkle with paprika. Cover and refrigerate 1 hour or overnight.

3 Preheat oven to 350°F. Bake strata about 45 minutes or until cheese is melted and bread is golden brown. Let stand 5 minutes before serving. Garnish with red bell pepper stars and fresh Italian parsley, if desired.　　*Makes 8 servings*

Nutrients per Serving:

Calories	297
(23% of calories from fat)	
Total Fat	7 g
Saturated Fat	3 g
Cholesterol	70 mg
Sodium	962 mg
Carbohydrate	38 g
Dietary Fiber	<1 g
Protein	18 g
Calcium	406 mg
Iron	143 mg
Vitamin A	160 RE
Vitamin C	1 mg

DIETARY EXCHANGES:
2 Starch/Bread, 1 Lean Meat, ½ Milk, 1 Fat

Health Note

To eliminate 53 mg of cholesterol per serving in this recipe, you may replace the whole eggs and egg whites with 1 cup egg substitute.

SEAFOOD PAELLA

Paella is considered the national dish of Spain, but varies from one region to another depending on the ingredients available. This version is most prevalent along the Spanish coast.

Nutrients per Serving:

Calories	357
(9% of calories from fat)	
Total Fat	4 g
Saturated Fat	1 g
Cholesterol	98 mg
Sodium	281 mg
Carbohydrate	46 g
Dietary Fiber	3 g
Protein	27 g
Calcium	99 mg
Iron	6 mg
Vitamin A	90 RE
Vitamin C	43 mg

DIETARY EXCHANGES:
2½ Starch/Bread, 2 Lean Meat, 2½ Vegetable

1 tablespoon olive oil
4 cloves garlic, minced
4½ cups finely chopped onions
2 cups uncooked long-grain white rice
2 cups clam juice
2 cups dry white wine
3 tablespoons fresh lemon juice
½ teaspoon paprika
½ teaspoon saffron or ground turmeric
¼ cup boiling water
1½ cups peeled and diced plum tomatoes
½ cup finely chopped fresh parsley
1 jar (8 ounces) roasted red peppers, drained, thinly sliced and divided
1 pound bay scallops, rinsed and drained
1½ cups frozen peas, thawed
10 clams, scrubbed
10 mussels, scrubbed
20 large shrimp (1 pound), shelled and deveined

1 Preheat oven to 375°F. Heat oil in large ovenproof skillet or paella pan over medium-low heat until hot. Add garlic and cook just until garlic sizzles. Add onions and rice; cook and stir 10 minutes or until onions are soft. Stir in clam juice, wine, lemon juice and paprika; mix well.

2 Combine saffron and boiling water in small bowl; stir until saffron is dissolved. Stir into onion mixture. Stir in tomatoes, parsley and half the red pepper. Bring to a boil over medium heat. Remove from heat; cover. Place on lowest shelf of oven. Bake 1 hour or until all liquid is absorbed.

3 Remove from oven; stir in scallops and peas. *Turn oven off;* return paella to oven. Steam clams and mussels 4 to 6 minutes, removing each as shells open. Discard any unopened clams or mussels. Steam shrimp 2 to 3 minutes *just* until shrimp turn pink and opaque.

4 To serve, remove paella from oven and arrange clams, mussels and shrimp on top. Garnish with remaining red pepper.

Makes 10 servings

SOUTHWESTERN BEEF AND BEAN LASAGNA

❖

This delicate one-dish meal is packed with protein from beans and lean beef without all the fat, so there's no need to skimp on the serving size. However, for lighter appetites and children, this variation to the Italian classic may easily be stretched to 10 servings.

❖

Nutrients per Serving:

Calories	416
(25% of calories from fat)	
Total Fat	12 g
Saturated Fat	4 g
Cholesterol	40 mg
Sodium	1270 mg
Carbohydrate	50 g
Dietary Fiber	5 g
Protein	30 g
Calcium	271 mg
Iron	3 mg
Vitamin A	262 RE
Vitamin C	36 mg

DIETARY EXCHANGES:
2½ Starch/Bread, 2 Lean Meat, 3 Vegetable, 1 Fat

½ pound extra lean ground beef
1 can (16 ounces) pinto beans, drained
1 teaspoon cumin seeds *or* ½ teaspoon ground cumin
1 teaspoon olive oil
1½ cups chopped onions
1 tablespoon seeded and minced jalapeño pepper
1 clove garlic, minced
4 cups no-salt-added tomato sauce
1 can (4 ounces) diced green chilies, undrained
2 teaspoons chili powder
1 teaspoon dried oregano leaves
1 container (8 ounces) nonfat cottage cheese
1½ cups (6 ounces) shredded reduced fat Cheddar cheese, divided
1 egg white
¼ cup chopped fresh cilantro
½ teaspoon salt
¼ teaspoon black pepper
8 ounces uncooked lasagna noodles
1 cup water

 Brown beef in large skillet. Drain off fat. Stir in beans; set aside. Place cumin seeds in large nonstick skillet. Cook and stir over medium heat 2 minutes or until fragrant (omit step if using ground). Remove from skillet. In same skillet, heat oil. Add onions, jalapeño and garlic; cook until onions are soft. Add tomato sauce, green chilies, chili powder, oregano and roasted cumin seeds or ground cumin. Bring to a boil; reduce heat. Simmer, uncovered, 20 minutes.

2 Preheat oven to 350°F. Combine cottage cheese, ½ cup Cheddar cheese, egg white, cilantro, salt and black pepper in medium bowl. Spray 13×9-inch baking pan with nonstick cooking spray. Cover bottom with ¾ cup tomato sauce mixture. Place layer of noodles on sauce. Spread half the beef mixture over noodles, then place another layer of noodles on top. Spread cheese mixture over noodles. Spread with remaining beef mixture. Layer with noodles. Pour remaining sauce mixture over all; sprinkle with remaining 1 cup Cheddar cheese. Pour water around edges. Cover tightly with foil. Bake 1 hour and 15 minutes or until pasta is tender. Cool 10 minutes before serving.

Makes 6 to 10 servings

Salads

GAZPACHO SALAD

This colorful and spicy salad features the same combination of tastes and textures found in the famous cold Mexican soup. Try it with freshly toasted Corn Tortilla Chips (page 182).

1½ cups peeled and coarsely chopped tomatoes*
1 cup peeled, seeded and diced cucumber
¾ cup chopped onion
½ cup chopped red bell pepper
½ cup fresh or frozen corn kernels, cooked and drained
1 tablespoon lime juice
1 tablespoon red wine vinegar
2 teaspoons water
1 teaspoon extra virgin olive oil
1 teaspoon minced fresh garlic
¼ teaspoon salt
¼ teaspoon black pepper
   Pinch ground red pepper
1 medium head romaine lettuce, torn into bite-sized pieces
1 cup peeled and diced jicama
½ cup fresh cilantro

 Combine tomatoes, cucumber, onion, bell pepper and corn in large bowl. Combine lime juice, vinegar, water, oil, garlic, salt, black pepper and ground red pepper in small bowl; whisk until well blended. Pour over tomato mixture; toss well. Cover and refrigerate several hours to allow flavors to blend.

2 Toss together lettuce, jicama and cilantro in another large bowl. Divide lettuce mixture evenly among 6 plates. Place ⅔ cup chilled tomato mixture on top of lettuce, spreading to edges.

Makes 6 servings

*To peel tomatoes easily, blanch in boiling water 30 seconds; immediately transfer to bowl of cold water, then peel.

Nutrients per Serving:

Calories	71
(14% of calories from fat)	
Total Fat	1 g
Saturated Fat	<1 g
Cholesterol	0 mg
Sodium	105 mg
Carbohydrate	14 g
Dietary Fiber	3 g
Protein	3 g
Calcium	51 mg
Iron	2 mg
Vitamin A	287 RE
Vitamin C	52 mg

DIETARY EXCHANGES:
3 Vegetable

GARDEN GREENS WITH FENNEL DRESSING

*The pine nuts add only
1 gram of fat to this salad;
however, if you prefer to
have only 23% of the calories
from fat, omit the nuts.
Eating greens is a great,
tasty way to get calcium
into your diet.*

DRESSING

½ teaspoon unflavored gelatin
2 tablespoons cold water
¼ cup boiling water
½ teaspoon salt
½ teaspoon sugar
¼ teaspoon dry mustard
⅛ teaspoon black pepper
¼ teaspoon anise extract *or* ground fennel seeds
1 tablespoon fresh lemon juice
¼ cup raspberry or wine vinegar
1¼ teaspoons walnut or canola oil

SALAD

1 head (10 ounces) Bibb lettuce, torn into bite-sized pieces
1 head (10 ounces) radicchio, torn into bite-sized pieces
1 bunch arugula (3 ounces), torn into bite-sized pieces
1 cup mache *or* spinach leaves, washed and torn into bite-sized pieces
1 fennel bulb (8 ounces), finely chopped (reserve fern for garnish)
1 tablespoon pine nuts, toasted

1 To prepare dressing, sprinkle gelatin over cold water in small bowl; let stand 1 minute to soften. Add boiling water; stir 2 minutes or until gelatin is completely dissolved. Add salt and sugar; stir until sugar is completely dissolved. Add all remaining dressing ingredients except oil; mix well. Slowly whisk in oil until well blended. Cover and refrigerate 2 hours or overnight. Shake well before using.

2 To prepare salad, place all salad ingredients except pine nuts in large bowl. Add dressing; toss until all leaves glisten. Divide salad among 6 chilled salad plates. Top each salad with ½ teaspoon pine nuts. Garnish with sprig of fennel fern, if desired.

Makes 6 servings

Nutrients per Serving:	
Calories	60
(30% of calories from fat)	
Total Fat	2 g
Saturated Fat	<1 g
Cholesterol	0 mg
Sodium	226 mg
Carbohydrate	9 g
Dietary Fiber	1 g
Protein	3 g
Calcium	94 mg
Iron	1 mg
Vitamin A	191 RE
Vitamin C	21 mg

DIETARY EXCHANGES:
1½ Vegetable, ½ Fat

GRILLED VEGETABLES

❖

Most vegetables require no preparation before grilling except slicing them into a uniform thickness. However, eggplant is better if sprinkled with a little salt after slicing and drained for an hour before grilling. This removes any bitterness. Not only are grilled vegetables excellent as a side dish, they are also great served over pasta, rice or beans.

❖

Nutrients per Serving:

Calories	34
(6% of calories from fat)	
Total Fat	<1 g
Saturated Fat	<1 g
Cholesterol	0 mg
Sodium	190 mg
Carbohydrate	8 g
Dietary Fiber	2 g
Protein	1 g
Calcium	24 mg
Iron	1 mg
Vitamin A	54 RE
Vitamin C	43 mg

DIETARY EXCHANGES:
1½ Vegetable

¼ cup minced fresh herbs, such as parsley, thyme, rosemary, oregano or basil
1 small eggplant (about ¾ pound), cut into ¼-inch-thick slices
½ teaspoon salt
  Nonstick cooking spray
1 *each* red, green and yellow bell pepper, quartered and seeded
2 zucchini, cut lengthwise into ¼-inch-thick slices
1 fennel bulb, cut lengthwise into ¼-inch-thick slices

1 Combine herbs of your choice in small bowl; let stand 3 hours or overnight.

2 Place eggplant in large colander over bowl; sprinkle with salt. Drain 1 hour.

3 Heat grill until coals are glowing red, but not flaming. Spray vegetables with cooking spray and sprinkle with herb mixture. Grill 10 to 15 minutes or until fork-tender and lightly browned on both sides. (Cooking times vary depending on vegetable; remove vegetables as they are done to avoid overcooking.)

Makes 6 servings

Variation: Cut vegetables into 1-inch cubes and thread onto skewers. Spray with cooking spray and sprinkle with herb mixture. Grill as directed above.

❖

Cook's Tip
Fennel is an anise-flavored, bulb-shaped vegetable with celerylike stems and feathery leaves. Both the base and stems can be eaten raw in salads, grilled or sautéed. The seeds and leaves can be used for seasoning food. Purchase clean, crisp bulbs with no sign of browning.

❖

MARINATED TOMATO SALAD

❖

This uniquely different salad takes full advantage of the colorful array of tomatoes available in the summer. During other seasons, you can make this salad with readily available plum tomatoes. The subtly seasoned marinade enhances the fabulous flavor of truly ripe tomatoes without masking it. This salad should be served at room temperature. Refrigerating tomatoes destroys their natural flavor and texture.

❖

MARINADE

1½ cups tarragon or white wine vinegar
½ teaspoon salt
¼ cup finely chopped shallots
2 tablespoons finely chopped chives
2 tablespoons fresh lemon juice
¼ teaspoon ground white pepper
2 tablespoons extra virgin olive oil

SALAD

6 plum tomatoes, quartered vertically
2 large yellow tomatoes, sliced horizontally into ½-inch slices
16 red cherry tomatoes, halved vertically
16 small yellow pear tomatoes, halved vertically

1 To prepare marinade, combine vinegar and salt in large bowl; stir until salt is completely dissolved. Add shallots, chives, lemon juice and white pepper; mix well. Slowly whisk in oil until smooth and well blended.

2 Add tomatoes to marinade; toss well. Cover and let stand at room temperature 2 to 3 hours.

3 To serve, place 3 plum tomato quarters on each of 8 salad plates. Add 2 slices yellow tomato, 4 cherry tomato halves and 4 pear tomato halves. Garnish each plate with sunflower sprouts, if desired. (Or, place all marinated tomatoes on large serving plate.)

Makes 8 servings

Nutrients per Serving:

Calories	56
(24% of calories from fat)	
Total Fat	2 g
Saturated Fat	<1 g
Cholesterol	0 mg
Sodium	64 mg
Carbohydrate	10 g
Dietary Fiber	2 g
Protein	2 g
Calcium	15 mg
Iron	1 mg
Vitamin A	145 RE
Vitamin C	40 mg

DIETARY EXCHANGES:
2 Vegetable

PASTA SALAD

❖

Spiral-shaped pastas work best for salads because they hold the dressing well. This vegetable-packed pasta salad is a wonderful side dish for Grilled Marinated chicken (page 200), but you may easily turn it into an entrée by adding cooked poultry or water-packed canned tuna. For an easy and delicious vegetarian entrée, add your favorite cooked beans.

❖

4 cups broccoli flowerets
2 cups carrot slices
1½ cups chopped tomatoes
½ cup chopped green onions with tops
½ pound spiral pasta, cooked and well drained
1 cup fat free mayonnaise
2 tablespoons white wine vinegar
1 tablespoon extra virgin olive oil
1 tablespoon minced fresh basil *or* 1 teaspoon dried basil leaves
2 teaspoons minced fresh oregano *or* ½ teaspoon dried oregano leaves
1 clove garlic, minced
1 teaspoon sugar
1 teaspoon dry mustard
¼ teaspoon *each* salt and black pepper
½ cup (2 ounces) freshly grated Romano cheese

1 Steam broccoli 3 minutes or until crisp-tender; immediately drain and run under cold water. Steam carrots 4 minutes or until crisp-tender; immediately drain and run under cold water. Combine broccoli, carrots, tomatoes, green onions and pasta in large bowl.

2 Combine all remaining ingredients except cheese in small bowl; blend well. Stir into pasta mixture. Add cheese; toss well. Refrigerate 3 hours or overnight to allow flavors to blend.
Makes 8 servings

Nutrients per Serving:

1¼ cups

Calories	215
(20% of calories from fat)	
Total Fat	5 g
Saturated Fat	2 g
Cholesterol	7 mg
Sodium	573 mg
Carbohydrate	35 g
Dietary Fiber	5 g
Protein	9 g
Calcium	138 mg
Iron	2 mg
Vitamin A	973 RE
Vitamin C	92 mg

DIETARY EXCHANGES:
1½ Starch/Bread,
2½ Vegetable, 1 Fat

STILTON SALAD DRESSING

❖

In this salad dressing, most of the cholesterol usually found in cheese dressings is missing by using tofu for texture and low fat cottage cheese for the lumps associated with the higher fat Stilton. Toasting the walnuts enhances their flavor enormously so that you can use fewer of them. Although adding 1 teaspoon of walnuts to each serving adds 2 grams of fat, it adds a lot of flavor.

❖

½ cup buttermilk
¼ cup silken firm tofu
2 ounces Stilton cheese
1 teaspoon fresh lemon juice
1 clove garlic, peeled
¼ teaspoon salt
⅛ teaspoon black pepper
2 tablespoons 1% low fat cottage cheese
  Romaine lettuce hearts, torn into bite-sized pieces (optional)
  Toasted chopped walnuts (optional)

1 Place buttermilk, tofu, Stilton cheese, lemon juice, garlic, salt and black pepper in blender or food processor; process until smooth. Pour mixture into small bowl and fold in cottage cheese. Store in airtight container and refrigerate 3 hours or overnight before serving. Serve with romaine lettuce and toasted walnuts, if desired.

Makes 6 servings

Nutrients per Serving:

Calories	51
(55% of calories from fat)	
Total Fat	3 g
Saturated Fat	2 g
Cholesterol	8 mg
Sodium	265 mg
Carbohydrate	2 g
Dietary Fiber	<1 g
Protein	4 g
Calcium	80 mg
Iron	<1 mg
Vitamin A	23 RE
Vitamin C	1 mg

DIETARY EXCHANGES:
½ Lean Meat, ½ Fat

❖

Cook's Tip

To toast walnuts, spread on baking sheet in a single layer. Bake in a preheated 350°F oven 5 to 10 minutes until lightly browned and fragrant. Watch carefully to avoid burning.

❖

Desserts

ALMOND BISCOTTI

❖

These no cholesterol, low fat Italian cookies are the perfect guilt free snack to satisfy any sweet tooth.

❖

¼ cup finely chopped almonds
½ cup sugar
2 tablespoons margarine
4 egg whites, lightly beaten
2 teaspoons almond extract
2 cups all-purpose flour
2 teaspoons baking powder
¼ teaspoon salt

1 Preheat oven to 375°F. Place almonds in small baking pan. Bake 7 to 8 minutes until golden brown. (Watch carefully to avoid burning.) Set aside.

2 Beat sugar and margarine in medium bowl with electric mixer until smooth. Add egg whites and almond extract; mix well. Combine flour, baking powder and salt in large bowl; mix well. Stir egg white mixture and almonds into flour mixture until well blended.

3 Spray two 9×5-inch loaf pans with nonstick cooking spray. Evenly divide dough between prepared pans. Spread dough evenly over bottoms of pans with wet fingertips. Bake 15 minutes or until knife inserted into centers comes out clean.

4 Remove from oven and turn out onto cutting board. As soon as loaves are cool enough to handle, cut each into 16 (½-inch-thick) slices. Place slices on baking sheets covered with parchment paper or sprayed with cooking spray. Bake 5 minutes; turn over. Bake 5 minutes more or until golden brown. Serve warm *or* cool completely and store in airtight container.

Makes 32 biscotti

Nutrients per Serving:

1 biscotti

Calories	56
(21% of calories from fat)	
Total Fat	1 g
Saturated Fat	<1 g
Cholesterol	0 mg
Sodium	53 mg
Carbohydrate	9 g
Dietary Fiber	<1 g
Protein	1 g
Calcium	8 mg
Iron	<1 mg
Vitamin A	9 RE
Vitamin C	<1 mg

DIETARY EXCHANGES:
½ Starch/Bread, ½ Fat

MARINATED POACHED PEACHES

❖

Serve these healthy goodies whole in dessert bowls paired with Almond Biscotti (page 220), or slice and fan on dessert plates with Vanilla Sauce (page 230).

❖

10 medium peaches
2 tablespoons whole allspice
10 cinnamon sticks
½ cup sugar

1 Place peaches in large saucepan or stockpot. Cover with water; add allspice and cinnamon. Bring to a boil over high heat. Boil 2 minutes; remove peaches and peel when cool enough to handle. Add sugar to poaching water and boil 5 minutes. Add peaches and simmer 2 minutes more.

2 Remove from heat; cool to room temperature in poaching liquid. Place peaches and liquid in airtight container. Refrigerate 3 hours or overnight. Cut into slices and garnish with fresh mint and raspberries, if desired. Serve cold.　　*Makes 10 servings*

Nutrients per Serving:

1 peach

Calories	83
(2% of calories from fat)	
Total Fat	<1 g
Saturated Fat	<1 g
Cholesterol	0 mg
Sodium	1 mg
Carbohydrate	22 g
Dietary Fiber	1 g
Protein	1 g
Calcium	29 mg
Iron	1 mg
Vitamin A	47 RE
Vitamin C	7 mg

DIETARY EXCHANGES:
1½ Fruit

❖

Cook's Tip

Ripen peaches at room temperature. When ripe, store in the refrigerator. Peaches are a great source of potassium, vitamin A and fiber.

❖

HONEY CARROT CAKE

❖

*The pineapple in this recipe
gives the cake a fabulous
flavor and also helps to keep
it moist without adding fat.
In addition, the frosting
contains almost no fat since
it is made with Neufchâtel
cheese, a lighter version of
cream cheese.*

❖

Nutrients per Serving:	
Calories	272
(29% of calories from fat)	
Total Fat	9 g
Saturated Fat	2 g
Cholesterol	22 mg
Sodium	112 mg
Carbohydrate	45 g
Dietary Fiber	1 g
Protein	4 g
Calcium	42 mg
Iron	1 mg
Vitamin A	623 RE
Vitamin C	3 mg

DIETARY EXCHANGES:
2½ Starch/Bread, ½ Fruit,
1½ Fat

2 cups all-purpose flour
2 teaspoons baking powder
1½ teaspoons ground cinnamon
1 cup firmly packed dark brown sugar
½ cup honey
⅓ cup canola oil
1 whole egg
3 egg whites
3 cups shredded carrots
1 can (8 ounces) crushed pineapple in juice, drained
¼ cup chopped toasted pecans
6 ounces Neufchâtel cheese, softened
¾ cup powdered sugar
1 tablespoon cornstarch
1½ teaspoons vanilla extract

1 Preheat oven to 350°F. Spray 13×9-inch baking pan with nonstick cooking spray; set aside. Combine flour, baking powder and cinnamon in small bowl; set aside. Beat together sugar, honey, oil, whole egg and egg whites in large bowl with electric mixer. Gradually beat flour mixture into sugar mixture on low speed until well blended. Stir in carrots, pineapple and pecans.

2 Pour batter into prepared pan. Bake 40 to 45 minutes until toothpick inserted into center comes out clean. Cool completely in pan on wire rack.

3 To prepare frosting, beat cheese, powdered sugar, cornstarch and vanilla in small bowl until smooth. Spread frosting over top of cake, reserving some frosting to tint with food coloring and pipe carrots for garnish, if desired. Store in refrigerator.

Makes 16 servings

Variation: Instead of folding pecans into batter, sprinkle over frosting for garnish.

FIRE AND ICE

❖

This whimsical, southwestern dessert is designed to represent all of the colors of the Mexican flag. It is a perfect finale for a fiesta and it's fun to decorate each serving with a little Mexican flag.

❖

Nutrients per Serving:

Calories	152
(11% of calories from fat)	
Total Fat	2 g
Saturated Fat	1 g
Cholesterol	7 mg
Sodium	58 mg
Carbohydrate	32 g
Dietary Fiber	3 g
Protein	4 g
Calcium	112 mg
Iron	<1 mg
Vitamin A	32 RE
Vitamin C	62 mg

DIETARY EXCHANGES:
1½ Starch/Bread, 1 Fruit

2 cups vanilla ice milk or low fat ice cream
2 teaspoons finely chopped jalapeño pepper
1 teaspoon grated lime peel, divided
1 cup water
¼ cup sugar
1 cup peeled and chopped kiwifruit
1 tablespoon lime juice
1 cup fresh raspberries

1 Soften ice milk slightly in small bowl. Stir in jalapeño and ½ teaspoon lime peel. Freeze until firm.

2 Combine water, sugar and remaining ½ teaspoon lime peel in small saucepan; bring to a boil. Boil, uncovered, 5 minutes or until reduced by about one-third. Remove from heat and cool to room temperature.

3 Place kiwifruit and lime juice in blender or food processor; process until blended. Stir in water mixture. Pour through fine strainer to remove kiwifruit seeds and lime peel, pressing liquid through strainer with back of spoon. Refrigerate kiwifruit mixture until cold.

4 Pour ¼ cup kiwifruit mixture into each of 6 chilled bowls. Scoop ⅓ cup jalapeño ice milk in center of each bowl. Sprinkle raspberries evenly on top. Garnish with lime peel strips, if desired.

Makes 6 servings

❖

Cook's Tip

Jalapeño peppers can sting and irritate the skin; wear plastic disposable gloves when handling peppers and do not touch eyes. To seed, cut peppers in half lengthwise. Remove seeds, membranes and stems with small paring knife.

❖

TEMPTING APPLE TRIFLES

❖

Just as Eve tempted Adam with an apple, you may find that this scrumptious dessert is truly the final touch to winning the lasting affection of that special someone in your life. . . especially when he or she learns that there are only 246 calories, 2 grams of fat and almost no cholesterol per serving in this rich-tasting trifle.

❖

Nutrients per Serving:

Calories	246
(6% of calories from fat)	
Total Fat	2 g
Saturated Fat	<1 g
Cholesterol	1 mg
Sodium	117 mg
Carbohydrate	53 g
Dietary Fiber	2 g
Protein	6 g
Calcium	104 mg
Iron	1 mg
Vitamin A	41 RE
Vitamin C	5 mg

DIETARY EXCHANGES:
2 Starch/Bread, 1½ Fruit

½ cup skim milk
1½ teaspoons cornstarch
4½ teaspoons dark brown sugar
1 egg white
½ teaspoon canola oil
½ teaspoon vanilla extract
½ teaspoon rum extract, divided
¼ cup unsweetened apple cider, divided
2 tablespoons raisins
½ teaspoon ground cinnamon
1 cup peeled and chopped Golden Delicious apple
1 cup ½-inch angel food cake cubes, divided

1 To prepare custard, combine milk and cornstarch in small heavy saucepan; stir until cornstarch is completely dissolved. Add brown sugar, egg white and oil; blend well. Slowly bring to a boil over medium-low heat until thickened, stirring constantly with whisk. Remove from heat; stir in vanilla and ¼ teaspoon rum extract. Set aside; cool completely.

2 Combine 2 tablespoons cider, raisins and cinnamon in medium saucepan; bring to a boil over medium-low heat. Add apple and cook until apple is fork-tender and all liquid has been absorbed, stirring frequently. Remove from heat; set aside to cool.

3 To assemble, place ¼ cup cake cubes in bottom of 2 small trifle or dessert dishes. Combine remaining 2 tablespoons cider and ¼ teaspoon rum extract in small bowl; mix well. Spoon 1½ teaspoons cider mixture over cake in each dish. Spoon ¼ of custard mixture over cake in each dish, then top each with ¼ cup cooked apple mixture. Repeat layers. Serve immediately. Garnish with fresh mint, if desired.

Makes 2 servings

COLD CHERRY MOUSSE WITH VANILLA SAUCE

Nutrients per Serving:

includes 2 tablespoons sauce

Calories	198
(25% of calories from fat)	
Total Fat	6 g
Saturated Fat	1 g
Cholesterol	5 mg
Sodium	64 mg
Carbohydrate	34 g
Dietary Fiber	1 g
Protein	4 g
Calcium	88 mg
Iron	1 mg
Vitamin A	99 RE
Vitamin C	5 mg

DIETARY EXCHANGES:
1½ Starch/Bread, 1 Fruit,
1 Fat

Nutrients per Serving:

1 tablespoon

Calories	25
(21% of calories from fat)	
Total Fat	1 g
Saturated Fat	<1 g
Cholesterol	2 mg
Sodium	12 mg
Carbohydrate	4 g
Dietary Fiber	0 g
Protein	1 g
Calcium	20 mg
Iron	<1 mg
Vitamin A	7 RE
Vitamin C	<1 mg

DIETARY EXCHANGES:
½ Fruit

1 envelope whipped topping mix
½ cup skim milk
½ teaspoon vanilla extract
2 envelopes unflavored gelatin
½ cup sugar
½ cup cold water
1 package (16 ounces) frozen unsweetened cherries, thawed, undrained and divided
1 tablespoon fresh lemon juice
½ teaspoon almond extract
¾ cup Vanilla Sauce (recipe follows)

1 Prepare whipped topping according to package directions using milk and vanilla; set aside. Combine gelatin and sugar in small saucepan; stir in water. Let stand 5 minutes to soften. Heat over low heat until gelatin is completely dissolved. Cool to room temperature.

2 Set aside 1 cup cherries without juice for garnish. Place remaining cherries and juice in blender. Add lemon juice, almond extract and gelatin mixture; process until blended. Fold cherry purée into whipped topping until no streaks of white show. Pour mixture into Bundt pan or ring mold. Refrigerate 4 hours or overnight until jelled.

3 To serve, unmold mousse onto large serving plate. Spoon remaining 1 cup cherries into center of mousse. Serve with Vanilla Sauce. Garnish with fresh mint, if desired.

Makes 6 servings

VANILLA SAUCE

4½ teaspoons cherry brandy *or* 1 teaspoon vanilla extract plus ½ teaspoon cherry extract
¾ cup melted vanilla ice milk or low fat ice cream, cooled

1 Stir brandy into ice milk in small bowl; blend well.   *Makes 12 servings*

Variations: You may vary the flavor just by trying different liqueurs or extracts. Try Grand Marnier in the sauce and pour over fresh berries. Amaretto in the sauce tastes great over sliced peaches. Add dark rum to the sauce and serve over sliced bananas.

FRESH APRICOT COBBLER

1 cup all-purpose flour
¼ cup granulated sugar
2 tablespoons instant nonfat dry milk powder
2 teaspoons baking powder
¼ teaspoon baking soda
¼ teaspoon salt
2 tablespoons canola oil
7 tablespoons buttermilk
½ cup firmly packed dark brown sugar
4½ teaspoons cornstarch
½ cup water
1½ pound ripe apricots, pits removed, quartered
　　Cinnamon Yogurt Topping (page 234)

1 Preheat oven to 400°F. Combine flour, granulated sugar, dry milk, baking powder, baking soda and salt in medium bowl. Stir in oil until mixture becomes crumbly. Add buttermilk and stir just until moistened.

2 Combine brown sugar, cornstarch and water in medium saucepan, stirring until cornstarch is dissolved. Cook over medium heat until thickened, stirring constantly. Add apricots; cook and stir about 3 minutes or until apricots are completely covered in sauce.

3 Pour into 8-inch square baking pan and immediately drop flour mixture in small spoonfuls on top of apricot mixture. Bake 25 minutes or until topping is lightly browned. Serve warm with Cinnamon Yogurt Topping, if desired.   *Makes 6 servings*

Nutrients per Serving:

without yogurt topping

Calories	293
(16% of calories from fat)	
Total Fat	5 g
Saturated Fat	1 g
Cholesterol	1 mg
Sodium	286 mg
Carbohydrate	58 g
Dietary Fiber	3 g
Protein	5 g
Calcium	93 mg
Iron	2 mg
Vitamin A	308 RE
Vitamin C	12 mg

DIETARY EXCHANGES:
2½ Starch/Bread, 1 Fruit,
1 Fat

❖

Nutrients per Serving:

with ½ cup yogurt topping

Calories	364
(13% of calories from fat)	
Total Fat	5 g
Saturated Fat	1 g
Cholesterol	2 mg
Sodium	332 mg
Carbohydrate	72 g
Dietary Fiber	3 g
Protein	9 g
Calcium	205 mg
Iron	2 mg
Vitamin A	329 RE
Vitamin C	13 mg

DIETARY EXCHANGES:
3 Starch/Bread, ½ Milk,
1 Fruit, 1 Fat

CINNAMON YOGURT TOPPING

❖

This melt-in-your-mouth dessert can certainly stand alone, but a dollop of it is fantastic on Fresh Apricot Cobbler (page 232). Because this yogurt has not actually been frozen and processed, all of its valuable bacteria are still active. It is best served soon after it is made. Recipe pictured on page 233.

❖

Nutrients per Serving:

½ cup

Calories	72
(1% of calories from fat)	
Total Fat	<1 g
Saturated Fat	<1 g
Cholesterol	1 mg
Sodium	46 mg
Carbohydrate	13 g
Dietary Fiber	0 g
Protein	4 g
Calcium	113 mg
Iron	<1 mg
Vitamin A	21 RE
Vitamin C	1 mg

DIETARY EXCHANGES:
½ Starch/Bread, ½ Milk

1 envelope unflavored gelatin
2 tablespoons cold water
¼ cup boiling water
1 cup plain nonfat yogurt
¼ cup instant nonfat dry milk powder
¼ cup sugar
¼ to ½ teaspoon ground cinnamon
1½ teaspoons vanilla extract
2 cups crushed ice

1 Sprinkle gelatin over cold water in medium bowl; let stand 1 minute to soften. Add boiling water; stir about 2 minutes or until gelatin is completely dissolved. Add yogurt and mix well. Refrigerate until jelled.

2 Place yogurt mixture in blender or food processor. Add all remaining ingredients; process until smooth. Serve immediately or cover and refrigerate.

Makes 6 servings

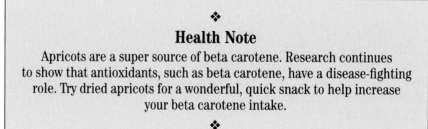

❖

Health Note

Apricots are a super source of beta carotene. Research continues to show that antioxidants, such as beta carotene, have a disease-fighting role. Try dried apricots for a wonderful, quick snack to help increase your beta carotene intake.

❖

INDEX

Personalized Nutrition Reference for Different Calorie Levels*

Daily Calorie Level	1,600	2,000	2,200	2,800
Total Fat	53 g	65 g	73 g	93 g
% of Calories from Fat	30%	30%	30%	30%
Saturated Fat	18 g	20 g	24 g	31 g
Carbohydrate	240 g	300 g	330 g	420 g
Protein	46 g**	50 g	55 g	70 g
Dietary Fiber	20 g***	25 g	25 g	32 g
Cholesterol	300 mg	300 mg	300 mg	300 mg
Sodium	2,400 mg	2,400 mg	2,400 mg	2,400 mg
Calcium	1,000 mg	1,000 mg	1,000 mg	1,000 mg
Iron	18 mg	18 mg	18 mg	18 mg
Vitamin A	1,000 RE	1,000 RE	1,000 RE	1,000 RE
Vitamin C	60 mg	60 mg	60 mg	60 mg

  * Numbers may be rounded
 ** 46 g is the minimum amount of protein recommended for all
    calorie levels below 1,800.
*** 20 g is the minimum amount of fiber recommended for all calorie
    levels below 2,000.

Note: These calorie levels may not apply to children or adolescents, who have varying calorie requirements. For specific advice concerning calorie levels, please consult a registered dietitian, qualified health professional or pediatrician.

VOLUME MEASUREMENTS (dry)

⅛ teaspoon = 0.5 mL
¼ teaspoon = 1 mL
½ teaspoon = 2 mL
¾ teaspoon = 4 mL
1 teaspoon = 5 mL
1 tablespoon = 15 mL
2 tablespoons = 30 mL
¼ cup = 60 mL
⅓ cup = 75 mL
½ cup = 125 mL
⅔ cup = 150 mL
¾ cup = 175 mL
1 cup = 250 mL
2 cups = 1 pint = 500 mL
3 cups = 750 mL
4 cups = 1 quart = 1 L

VOLUME MEASUREMENTS (fluid)

1 fluid ounce (2 tablespoons) = 30 mL
4 fluid ounces (½ cup) = 125 mL
8 fluid ounces (1 cup) = 250 mL
12 fluid ounces (1½ cups) = 375 mL
16 fluid ounces (2 cups) = 500 mL

WEIGHTS (mass)

½ ounce = 15 g
1 ounce = 30 g
3 ounces = 90 g
4 ounces = 120 g
8 ounces = 225 g
10 ounces = 285 g
12 ounces = 360 g
16 ounces = 1 pound = 450 g

DIMENSIONS

1/16 inch = 2 mm
⅛ inch = 3 mm
¼ inch = 6 mm
½ inch = 1.5 cm
¾ inch = 2 cm
1 inch = 2.5 cm

OVEN TEMPERATURES

250°F = 120°C
275°F = 140°C
300°F = 150°C
325°F = 160°C
350°F = 180°C
375°F = 190°C
400°F = 200°C
425°F = 220°C
450°F = 230°C

BAKING PAN SIZES

Utensil	Size in Inches/Quarts	Metric Volume	Size in Centimeters
Baking or Cake Pan (square or rectangular)	8×8×2	2 L	20×20×5
	9×9×2	2.5 L	22×22×5
	12×8×2	3 L	30×20×5
	13×9×2	3.5 L	33×23×5
Loaf Pan	8×4×3	1.5 L	20×10×7
	9×5×3	2 L	23×13×7
Round Layer Cake Pan	8×1½	1.2 L	20×4
	9×1½	1.5 L	23×4
Pie Plate	8×1¼	750 mL	20×3
	9×1¼	1 L	23×3
Baking Dish or Casserole	1 quart	1 L	—
	1½ quart	1.5 L	—
	2 quart	2 L	—